THE POETRY FRIDAY ANTHOLOGY

FOR

CELEBRATIONS

HOLIDAY POEMS FOR THE WHOLE YEAR IN ENGLISH AND SPANISH

156 POEMS IN ENGLISH
156 POEMS IN SPANISH

115 POETS

compiled by

SYLVIA VARDELL AND JANET WONG

pomelo ✳ books

POETRY ANTHOLOGIES
COMPILED BY VARDELL AND WONG

THE POETRY FRIDAY ANTHOLOGY
Teacher Edition (Grades K-5)
Common Core version or *TEKS version*

THE POETRY FRIDAY ANTHOLOGY FOR MIDDLE SCHOOL
Teacher Edition (Grades 6-8)
Common Core version or *TEKS version*

THE POETRY FRIDAY ANTHOLOGY FOR SCIENCE
Teacher Edition (Grades K-5)
with a supplemental TEKS Guide available

THE POETRY OF SCIENCE:
THE POETRY FRIDAY ANTHOLOGY FOR SCIENCE FOR KIDS
An illustrated companion book to the Teacher/Librarian Edition with 30 Bonus Poems

THE POETRY FRIDAY ANTHOLOGY FOR CELEBRATIONS
Teacher/Librarian Edition
Student Edition

YOU JUST WAIT:
A POETRY FRIDAY POWER BOOK
A creative writing journal for tweens and teens

This book is dedicated to the memory of Lettie K. Albright,
colleague, friend & diversity advocate

and to the teachers, librarians, and administrators who have embraced
The Poetry Friday Anthology series

with special thanks to our Spanish language translators, consultants, and readers:
Alma Flor Ada, F. Isabel Campoy, and Liliana Cosentino;
Jennifer Barillas, Jenny Barillas, David Bowles, and Julie Larios;
Cynthia Alaniz, Consuelo Avila, Silvia Zulema Bewley, Patrina Garza,
Xelena Gonzalez, Brenda Linares, Juanita Vega, and Karim Zomar

and appreciation to Renée M. LaTulippe and Emily Vardell
for editorial assistance and research

Joy Acey
Alma Flor Ada
Francisco X. Alarcón
Jorge Argueta
Sandy Asher
Jeannine Atkins
Brod Bagert
Bruce Balan
Ibtisam Barakat
Michelle Heidenrich Barnes
Doraine Bennett
Carmen T. Bernier-Grand
Robyn Hood Black
Susan Blackaby
Merry Bradshaw
Joseph Bruchac
Stephanie Calmenson
Robyn Campbell
F. Isabel Campoy
Nancy White Carlstrom
Andrea Cheng
Kate Coombs
Cynthia Cotten
Kristy Dempsey
Rebecca Kai Dotlich
Linda Dryfhout
Shirley Duke
Margarita Engle
Matt Forrest Esenwine
Kelly Ramsdell Fineman
Carrie Finison
Nancy Bo Flood
Douglas Florian
Betsy Franco
Carole Gerber
Charles Ghigna
Cynthia Grady
Joan Bransfield Graham

Nikki Grimes
Lorie Ann Grover
Monica Gunning
Mary Lee Hahn
Avis Harley
David L. Harrison
Juanita Havill
Jane Heitman Healy
Georgia Heard
Stephanie Hemphill
Esther Hershenhorn
Sara Holbrook
Carol-Ann Hoyte
Jacqueline Jules
Bobbi Katz
Penny Parker Klostermann
Uma Krishnaswami
Michele Krueger
Julie Larios
Irene Latham
Renée M. LaTulippe
B.J. Lee
Neal Levin
Suzy Levinson
J. Patrick Lewis
Grace Lin
George Ella Lyon
Jone Rush MacCulloch
JoAnn Early Macken
Bridget Magee
Libby Martinez
Diane Mayr
Pat Mora
Diana Murray
Kenn Nesbitt
Lesléa Newman
Eric Ode
Linda Sue Park
Jane Lichtenberger Patton

Ann Whitford Paul
Jack Prelutsky
Mary Quattlebaum
Bob Raczka
Debbie Reese
Heidi Bee Roemer
Caroline Starr Rose
Michael J. Rosen
Deborah Ruddell
Laura Purdie Salas
René Saldaña, Jr.
Michael Salinger
Michelle Schaub
Robert Schechter
Ted Scheu
Joyce Sidman
Buffy Silverman
Marilyn Singer
Ken Slesarik
Eileen Spinelli
Elizabeth Steinglass
Tricia Stohr-Hunt
Anastasia Suen
Susan Marie Swanson
Rose Ann Tahe
Holly Thompson
Patricia Toht
Linda Kulp Trout
Amy Ludwig VanDerwater
Lee Wardlaw
Charles Waters
April Halprin Wayland
Tamera Will Wissinger
Steven Withrow
Allan Wolf
Virginia Euwer Wolff
Janet Wong
Jane Yolen

LIST OF CELEBRATIONS

JANUARY

January	National Soup Month	10
January	National Braille Literacy Month	11
January 1	New Year's Day	12
January 5	National Bird Day	13
January 6	Three Kings Day	14
2nd week in Jan	National Pizza Week	15
January 15	National Hat Day	16
mid-Jan to Feb	100th Day of School	17
3rd Monday in Jan	Martin Luther King, Jr. Day	18
January 19	National Popcorn Day	19
January 24	National Compliment Day	20
January 29	National Puzzle Day	21
January	Birthdays and Baby Days	22

FEBRUARY

late Jan to mid-Feb	Lunar New Year	23
February	Black History Month	24
early February	Super Bowl Sunday	25
February 2	Groundhog Day	26
mid-February	Carnival	27
2nd week in Feb	Random Acts of Kindness Week	28
February 14	Valentine's Day	29
3rd Monday in Feb	Presidents' Day	30
February 21	International Mother Language Day	31
February 22	World Thinking Day	32
mid- to late Feb	National Engineers Week	33
February 27	International Polar Bear Day	34
February	Birthdays and Baby Days	35

 PUT A ★ NEXT TO YOUR FAVORITE CELEBRATIONS

MARCH

March	National Women's History Month	36
1st week in March	Nat'l Write a Letter of Appreciation Day	37
March 2	Read Across America Day	38
March 7	National Cereal Day	39
2nd Sun in March	Daylight Saving Time Begins	40
mid-March	World Folktales and Fables Week	41
March 17	St. Patrick's Day	42
March 20/21	First Day of Spring	43
March 22	World Water Day	44
mid-Mar to mid-April	Passover	45
mid-Mar to mid-April	Easter	46
late Mar to early April	Baseball's Opening Day	47
March	Birthdays and Baby Days	48

APRIL

April	National Poetry Month	49
April	Arab American Heritage Month	50
April 2	International Children's Book Day	51
April 7	Metric System Day	52
early to mid-April	Week of the Young Child	53
mid-April	National Library Week	54
April 12	D.E.A.R. Day	55
3rd week in April	National Coin Week	56
April 22	Earth Day	57
late April	Poem in Your Pocket Day	58
April 29	International Dance Day	59
April 30	Día/Children's Day, Book Day	60
April	Birthdays and Baby Days	61

MAY

May	Asian Pacific Islander Heritage Month	62
May	National Photo Month	63
May	National Bike Month	64
May	National Physical Fitness and Sports Month	65
1st week in May	National Pet Week	66
1st week in May	National Teacher Appreciation Week	67
1st Sunday in May	World Laughter Day	68
May 8	World Red Cross Day	69
early May	Children's Book Week	70
2nd Sunday in May	Mother's Day	71
mid-May	National Etiquette Week	72
May 28	World Hunger Day	73
May	Birthdays and Baby Days	74

JUNE

May to June	Graduation	75
June	National Camping Month	76
June	National Fresh Fruit & Vegetables Month	77
June	National Zoo and Aquarium Month	78
June	Celebrate Summer Reading Month	79
June 6	National Yo-Yo Day	80
June 14	Flag Day	81
3rd Sunday in June	Father's Day	82
3rd Thursday in June	National Dump the Pump Day	83
June 19	Juneteenth	84
June 20/21	First Day of Summer	85
Last Sunday in June	Gay Pride Day	86
June	Birthdays and Baby Days	87

JULY

June to September	End of Ramadan	88
July	National Picnic Month	89
July 2	Halfway Day	90
July 4	Independence Day	91
July 8	Video Games Day	92
July 12	Paper Bag Day	93
mid-July to August	Obon	94
July 20	Blessing of the Boats	95
July 21	National Moon Walk Day	96
July 22	National Hammock Day	97
3rd Sunday in July	National Ice Cream Day	98
July 30	International Day of Friendship	99
July	Birthdays and Baby Days	100

AUGUST

August	Family Fun Month	101
early August	National Farmers' Market Week	102
August 3	Watermelon Day	103
August 3	Birthday of the NBA	104
August 8	Dollar Day	105
late June to mid-Aug	Shark Week	106
August 12	World Elephant Day	107
mid-Aug to Sept	First Day of School	108
August 16	National Tell a Joke Day	109
August 17	National Thrift Shop Day	110
August 19	National Aviation Day	111
August 24	National Waffle Day	112
August	Birthdays and Baby Days	113

SEPTEMBER

September	National Guide Dog Month	114
1st Sunday in Sept	Grandparents Day	115
September 10	Good Neighbor Day	116
mid-Sept to Oct	National Hispanic Heritage Month	117
mid-Sept to Oct	Mid-Autumn Moon Festival	118
mid-Sept to Oct	Tashlich (Rosh Hashanah)	119
September 16	National Blended Family Day	120
September 17	Constitution Day, Citizenship Day	121
September 19	International Talk Like a Pirate Day	122
September 22	Band-Aid Day	123
September 22/23	First Day of Fall	124
late Sept to late Oct	Dashain Festival	125
September	Birthdays and Baby Days	126

OCTOBER

October	International Dinosaur Month	127
October	National Roller Skating Month	128
October 1	International Music Day	129
2nd week in Oct	National Fire Prevention Week	130
2nd Friday in Oct	World Egg Day	131
October 14	National Dessert Day	132
October 15	Global Hand Washing Day	133
October 16	World Bread Day	134
October 16	Dictionary Day	135
October 17	National Pasta Day	136
mid-Oct to Nov	Diwali	137
October 31	Halloween	138
October	Birthdays and Baby Days	139

NOVEMBER

November	Native American Heritage Month	140
1st Tues in Nov	National Family Literacy Day	141
1st Sat in Nov	Election Day	142
November 1	International Games Day	143
November 1/2	Day of the Dead	144
November 3	National Sandwich Day	145
November 11	Veterans Day	146
mid-November	Guinness World Records Day	147
November 15	America Recycles Day	148
November 16	Button Day	149
Sat before Thanksgiving	National Adoption Day	150
4th Thurs in Nov	Thanksgiving	151
November	Birthdays and Baby Days	152

DECEMBER

December	Chanukah	153
December 3	Int'l Day of Persons with Disabilities	154
December 4	National Cookie Day	155
December 4	Wildlife Conservation Day	156
December 10	Dewey Decimal Day	157
December 12/13	National Cocoa Day	158
December 21	National Flashlight Day	159
December 21/22	First Day of Winter	160
December 25	Christmas	161
December 26	Boxing Day	162
Dec 26–Jan 1	Kwanzaa	163
December 31	New Year's Eve	164
December	Birthdays and Baby Days	165

THE POET CELEBRATES NATIONAL SOUP MONTH.
by Eileen Spinelli

Alphabet soup
is a favorite treat—
a soup to write poems in
as well as to eat.

LA POETISA CELEBRA EL MES NACIONAL DE LA SOPA.
basado en "The Poet Celebrates National Soup Month."
por Eileen Spinelli

La sopa de letras
es mi comida preferida—
una sopa para escribir poemas
y también para comer.

READING BRAILLE
by Steven Withrow

I sail my fingerships
Over a paper sea
I do not see

I sail my fingerships
Across a dotted alphabet
Shaped like wave caps

Forward and back
I do not stop
Until I touch bottom

Of the great, wide page.

LEER EN BRAILLE
basado en "Reading Braille"
por Steven Withrow

Navego el barco de mis dedos
Sobre un mar de papel
Que no veo

Navego el barco de mis dedos
A través del alfabeto de puntos
Con forma de cresta

Hacia adelante y hacia atrás
No me detengo
Hasta que toco el final

De la página grande y ancha.

NEW YEAR IS HERE
by Kenn Nesbitt

New Year is here!
Let's shout.
Let's cheer!
Yippee! Yahoo!
We start anew.
New dreams to chase.
New goals to face.
New plans to make.
New paths to take.
New skills to learn.
New stars to earn.
New hopes.
New prayers.
New loves.
New cares.
New facts to know.
Can't wait. Let's go!
Let's shout!
Let's cheer!
It's here! New Year!

LLEGÓ EL AÑO NUEVO
basado en "New Year Is Here"
por Kenn Nesbitt

¡Llegó el Año Nuevo!
¡Gritemos!
¡Brindemos!
¡Viva! ¡Hurra! ¡Hurra!
¡Que todo lo nuevo ocurra!
Nuevos sueños por soñar.
Nuevas metas por alcanzar.
Nuevos planes por hacer.
Nuevos caminos por ver.
Nuevas destrezas aprenderemos.
Nuevas estrellas ganaremos.
Nuevas ilusiones.
Nuevas oraciones.
Nuevos seres amados.
Nuevos cuidados.
Nuevos conocimientos.
¡No perdamos ni un momento!
¡Gritemos!
¡Brindemos!
¡Llegó el Año Nuevo!

I CAN HELP!
by Margarita Engle

My mother is knitting a pretty nest
so that rescued baby birds
will have a place to rest.

Someday I'll learn how to knit nests too,
but today I'll help by watching as quietly
as a little egg.

¡YO PUEDO AYUDAR!
por Margarita Engle

Mi mamá está tejiendo un nido lindo
para que los pajaritos rescatados
tengan un lugar para descansar.

Algún día voy a aprender a tejer nidos,
pero hoy puedo ayudar mirando tan calladito
como un huevito.

THREE KINGS DAY
by Carmen T. Bernier-Grand

We hear the story:
Three Wise Kings from the East
went to visit Jesus
and left Him three gifts.

We fill up shoeboxes with grass,
fill up bowls with water
for the Three Kings' camels
to eat and to drink.

Shoeboxes and bowls under beds,
we try to peek but fall asleep,
until kings and camels
have come and gone.

Trails of grass on the floor.
The water's gone, too!
Inside of each shoebox:
three gifts from Three Wise Kings.

TRES REYES MAGOS
por Carmen T. Bernier-Grand

Escuchamos el cuento:
Tres Reyes Magos del Oriente
fueron a ver al niño Jesús
y le dejaron tres regalos.

Llenamos de hierba las cajas de zapatos,
Llenamos de agua platos hondos
para que los camellos de los Santos Reyes
tengan algo de comer y beber.

Cajas y platos bajo las camas,
queremos espiar, pero nos quedamos dormidos
hasta que los reyes y sus camellos
han venido y se han ido.

Hay rastros de hierba por todo el piso.
¡Los platos están secos!
En cada caja encontramos tres regalos
que nos han dejado los Tres Reyes Magos.

PIZZA WEEK MENU
by Michelle Schaub

Monday: pepperoni
Tuesday: deep dish cheese
Wednesday: thin crust with the works,
no anchovies please!
Thursday: spinach-mushroom
Friday: meat supreme
Saturday: dessert-style
topped with fresh whipped cream!
Sunday: let's all make our own,
each pie will be unique!
Seven days of pizza—
that's one delicious week!

MENÚ SEMANAL DE PIZZA
basado en "Pizza Week Menu"
por Michelle Schaub

Lunes: de salame llena
Martes: gruesa con queso
Miércoles: delgada y completa,
¡pero anchoas no quiero!
Jueves: espinaca y champiñones
Viernes: suprema de carne a montones
Sábado: pizza dulce, cocida
¡cubierta de crema batida!
Domingo: ¡Hagamos nuestra fantasía,
única y sabrosa!
Pizza los siete días—
¡semana deliciosa!

HATS OFF TO HAT DAY
by Joan Bransfield Graham

Your hat can be
tall, skinny, wide,
perched on your head,
with a *tilt* down the side,
a baseball cap—what shall it be?
Show off your p e r s o n a l i t y !

QUÍTATE EL SOMBRERO POR EL DÍA DEL SOMBRERO
basado en "Hats Off to Hat Day"
por Joan Bransfield Graham

Tu sombrero puede ser alto,
bajo, angosto, un poco ancho,
derechito en la cabeza colocado
o también algo *inclinado* hacia un costado.
¿Una gorra de béisbol? ¿Qué será, qué será?
¡Muestra con ganas tu p e r s o n a l i d a d!

MY 100TH DAY COLLECTION
by Betsy Franco

I could line up
one hundred coins

or stack
one hundred blocks.

I could collect
one hundred nuts

or string
one hundred beads.

But I think I'll plant
one hundred seeds

and grow one hundred
TREATS!

MI COLECCIÓN DEL CENTÉSIMO DÍA
basado en "My 100th Day Collection" por Betsy Franco

Podría alinear
cien monedas

o apilar
cien bloques.

Podría recolectar
cien nueces

o atar
cien cuentas.

Pero plantaré
cien semillas,

¡y crecerán cien
DELICIAS!

MARTIN'S BIRTHDAY
by Nikki Grimes

Let's put candles on
Martin's cake and shake hands and
keep his dream alive.

EL CUMPLEAÑOS DE MARTIN
basado en "Martin's Birthday"
por Nikki Grimes

Vamos a ponerle velas
al pastel de Martin y tendernos las manos y
mantener vivo su sueño.

POPCORN PARTY
by Mary Quattlebaum

Pit pat pit
Kernels sit.

Pit pat   POP
Kernels hop!
They BOP and tumble,
flounce and fling.
Hop-hop! Pop-POP!
Pit-POP-PING
then
pit   pat
POP
the
hopping
slowly
starts
to
stop.

What a lot
of popcorn popped!

FIESTA DE PALOMITAS DE MAÍZ
basado en "Popcorn Party"
por Mary Quattlebaum

Pim pam pim
se pone el maíz.

Pim pam   POM
¡El maíz saltó!
Baila y da vueltas,
se hincha y hace piruetas.
¡Arriba, arriba! ¡Pom-POM!
Pim-POM-PIM
y después
pim   pam
POM
el
salto
de
a poco
se
terminó.

¡Un sin fin
de palomitas de maíz!

COMPLIMENT CHAIN
by Mary Lee Hahn

Your two small words
Good job!
filled me up.
I sat straighter in my chair.
I *had* worked hard.
And you noticed.

My friend
is bent over his paper.
His pencil moves slowly, carefully.
I say two small words,
Good job!
And watch him sit up straight.

CADENA DE CUMPLIDOS
basado en "Compliment Chain"
por Mary Lee Hahn

Tus dos palabras sencillas
¡Muy bien!
me llenaron de felicidad.
Me enderecé en la silla.
Sí que me había esforzado.
Y te diste cuenta.

Mi amigo, preocupado,
sobre la hoja de papel rayado,
mueve el lápiz despacio, con cuidado.
Le digo dos palabras sencillas,
¡Muy bien!
Y lo veo enderezarse en la silla.

100 PIECES
by Kristy Dempsey

Piece by piece,
bit by bit,
try them all
to find a fit.

First the edges,
then between,
filling in
a puzzling scene.

100 PIEZAS
basado en "100 Pieces"
por Kristy Dempsey

Pieza a pieza,
poquito a poco,
todas tratan
de encajar.

Primero, los bordes,
después, entre ellos,
así se completa
el rompecabezas.

BIRTHDAY TANKA
by Joyce Sidman

Birthdays begin
inside, when you realize
you are the gift
you want to keep giving
to everyone you love.

TANKA DE CUMPLEAÑOS
basado en "Birthday Tanka"
por Joyce Sidman

Tu cumpleaños comienza
dentro de ti, cuando comprendes
que tú eres el regalo
que quieres seguir dando
a los que amas.

NEW YEAR CHEER
by Linda Sue Park

"I like your dress!"
  "I like your vest!"
We look so fine,
  we look the best!

Our grandma's here.
  We're going to bow.
We've practiced lots,
  so we know how!

Who's bowing first?
  I will, I will!
A perfect bow—
  a dollar bill!

Note: To celebrate the Lunar New Year in Korea, children dress in colorful traditional clothing, called han-bok. They bow before their elders and receive gifts of money.

VIVA EL DÍA DE AÑO NUEVO
basado en "New Year Cheer"
por Linda Sue Park

—¡Me gusta tu vestido!
  —¡Me gusta tu chaleco!
¡Lucimos tan bien,
  lucimos gloriosos!

Nuestra abuelita está aquí.
  Vamos a inclinarnos.
¡Como hemos practicado mucho,
  sabemos hacerlo!

¿Quién se inclina primero?
  ¡Lo haré yo, lo haré yo!
Una reverencia perfecta—
  ¡un dólar en la mano!

Nota: Para celebrar el Año Nuevo Lunar en Corea, los niños se visten con los coloridos trajes tradicionales, llamados *hanbok*. Se inclinan ante los ancianos y reciben dinero de regalo.

BLACK HISTORY MONTH
by Charles Waters

Its mission: a month-long tradition
of African-American pride.
We celebrate brothers and sisters
who ended the racial divide.

MES DE LA HISTORIA AFROAMERICANA
basado en "Black History Month"
por Charles Waters

Su misión: un mes de larga tradición
de orgullo afroamericano.
Celebramos a los hermanos y las hermanas
que acabaron con la división racial.

LET'S READ
SOME POEMS
BY
LANGSTON HUGHES!

SUPER BOWL SUNDAY
by Jone Rush MacCulloch

On football's holiday
we wear team colors

We yell and cheer
at the television

We laugh together
at silly commercials

We crunch chips,
eat pizza and chili

We jump
up
  and
     down
when our team
makes the winning

TOUCHDOWN!

DOMINGO DEL SUPERTAZÓN
basado en "Super Bowl Sunday"
por Jone Rush MacCulloch

Los domingos de fútbol americano
usamos los colores de los equipos

Gritamos y alentamos
frente a la tele

Reímos juntos
de tontos anuncios

Comemos papitas,
comemos pizza y *chili*

Saltamos
arriba
    y
     abajo
cuando nuestro equipo
anota un

¡TOUCHDOWN!

MR. GROUNDHOG
by Jane Yolen

He's sometimes cranky,
always shy,
but he's the forest's
Weather Guy.

So on this day,
and in this crowd,
he says his forecast
right out loud.

Sees winter's shadow
on the wing,
looks all around
and calls it Spring.

EL SEÑOR MARMOTA
basado en "Mr. Groundhog"
por Jane Yolen

A veces gruñoso,
siempre vergonzoso,
pero es el meteorólogo
del bosque.

Así que en este día,
y con esta multitud,
dirá el pronóstico
en voz alta.

Ve volar
la sombra del invierno,
mira alrededor
y la llama primavera.

CARNIVAL TUESDAY
by Francisco X. Alarcón

every year my feet
look forward to
this special day

Mardi Gras
that in French
is "Fat Tuesday"—

if all Tuesdays
were just like
Carnival Tuesday

my feet would dance
forever to the drum
beat of my heart

MARTES DE CARNAVAL
por Francisco X. Alarcón

cada año mis pies
esperan ansiosos
este día especial

Mardi Gras
que en francés
es "Martes Gordo"—

si todos los martes
fueran igualitos
al Martes de Carnaval

mis pies bailarían
siempre al compás
tambor de mi corazón

HOW TO LOVE YOUR LITTLE CORNER
OF THE WORLD
by Eileen Spinelli

Help a neighbor.
Plant a tree.
Hug your friends
and family.
Be kind to pets.
Feed the birds.
Use your *please*
and *thank you* words.
Share a book.
Take a walk.
Someone's lonely?
Stop and talk.

CÓMO AMAR TU PEQUEÑO RINCÓN
DEL MUNDO
basado en "How to Love Your Little Corner of the World"
por Eileen Spinelli

Ayuda a un vecino.
Planta un árbol.
Abraza a tus amigos
y a tu familia.
Se gentil con las mascotas.
Da de comer a las aves.
Pide siempre *por favor*,
no dejes de dar las *gracias*.
Comparte un libro.
Y si sales a pasear
y ves que alguien está solo,
detente para conversar.

BILINGUAL DAISY
by F. Isabel Campoy

Do you love me?
Yes.
Do you love me?
No.
Do you love me?
Sí.
Do you love me?
No.
Do you love me?
¡Sí, sí, ¡te quiero!

MARGARITA BILINGÜE
por F. Isabel Campoy

¿Me quieres?
Sí.
¿Me quieres?
No.
¿Me quieres?
Yes.
¿Me quieres?
No.
¿Me quieres?
Yes, yes, I love you!

PRESIDENTS' DAY
by Bobbi Katz

In February, dark and gray,
we celebrate a holiday
to honor two great presidents.
Their influence was so immense.

George Washington, first president,
had a new office to invent.
There'd been kings and generals, too,
but a president—was something new!

Abe Lincoln knew there could not be
justice for all with slavery.
The United States would not succeed
if states that wished could just secede.

They kept our country strong and free.
They took care of democracy!
So in February, dark and gray,
we celebrate their holiday.

DÍA DE LOS PRESIDENTES
basado en "Presidents' Day" por Bobbi Katz

En febrero, oscuro y gris,
celebramos una fiesta
en honor a dos grandes presidentes.
Su influencia fue tan inmensa.

George Washington, el primer presidente,
tuvo que inventar su nueva función.
Ya había reyes y generales,
¡pero presidente, era algo nuevo!

Abe Lincoln sabía que no habría
justicia para todos si había esclavitud.
Los Estados Unidos no triunfarían
si podían separarse los estados que querían.

Ellos conservaron fuerte y libre a nuestro país.
¡Cuidaron de la democracia!
Por eso, en febrero, oscuro y gris,
celebramos esta fiesta patria.

BILINGUAL
by Alma Flor Ada

Because I speak Spanish
I can listen to my grandmother's stories
and say *familia, madre, amor.*
Because I speak English
I can learn from my teacher
and say **I love school**.
Because I am bilingual
I can read *libros* and **books**,
I have *amigos* and **friends**,
enjoy *canciones* and **songs**,
juegos and **games**
and have twice as much fun.
And someday,
because I speak two languages,
I will be able to do twice as much
to help twice as many people
and be twice as good in what I do.

BILINGÜE
por Alma Flor Ada

Porque hablo español
puedo escuchar los cuentos de abuelita
y decir **familia, madre, amor.**
Porque hablo inglés
puedo aprender de mi maestra
y decir *I love school.*
Porque soy bilingüe
puedo leer **libros** y *books*,
tengo **amigos** y *friends*,
disfruto **canciones** y *songs*,
juegos y *games*
¡y me divierto el doble!
Y algún día,
porque hablo dos idiomas,
podré hacer doble esfuerzo
para ayudar al doble de personas
y lo haré todo el doble de bien.

GAMES!   ¡JUEGOS!

THINKING ABOUT WORLD THINKING DAY
by Michelle Heidenrich Barnes

We are Girl Scout Troop 1520:
ten girls from a family of ten million.
Around the world, we join together—
across Egyptian deserts,
the rainforests of Guyana,
and Australian bushland.
We taste Irish soda bread,
Indian dal,
and fresh coconut from Fiji.
We learn customs and crafts,
games and traditions,
and explore how we are different,
yet very much the same.
We make a friendship circle
with our sisters across borders,
and promise each other
to make the world a better place.

PENSAR EN EL DÍA MUNDIAL DEL PENSAMIENTO
basado en "Thinking about World Thinking Day"
por Michelle Heidenrich Barnes

Somos la Tropa de Niñas Exploradoras 1520:
diez niñas de una familia de diez millones.
Estamos unidas en todo el mundo,
a través de los desiertos egipcios,
la selva tropical de Guyana
y la sabana australiana.
Probamos pan de soda irlandés,
dal de la India
y cocos frescos de Fiji.
Aprendemos costumbres y artesanías,
juegos y tradiciones,
y exploramos lo diferente que somos
y al mismo tiempo tan iguales.
Formamos un círculo de amistad
con nuestras hermanas, más allá de las fronteras,
y nos prometemos
hacer del mundo un lugar mejor.

ON NATIONAL ENGINEERS WEEK
by Suzy Levinson

Who designs a building that's
so tall it scrapes the sky?
And the airplanes high above . . .
which seem too big to fly?

Who draws up the plans for stuff
like toasters and TVs?
How about computer chips,
bikes, and water skis?

Who creates things, big and small,
that we use every day?
The answer: engineers, of course!
This week's for them—hooray!

EN LA SEMANA NACIONAL DE LOS INGENIEROS
basado en "On National Engineers Week"
por Suzy Levinson

¿Quiénes diseñan edificios tan altos
que rozan el cielo?
¿Y aviones que, allá arriba . . .
parecen demasiado grandes para volar?

¿Quiénes dibujan los planos para cosas
como tostadoras y televisores?
¿Qué tal los chips de las computadoras,
las bicicletas y los esquíes acuáticos?

¿Quiénes crean las cosas, grandes y pequeñas,
que usamos todos los días?
La respuesta: ¡los ingenieros, por supuesto!
Esta semana es para ellos. ¡Hurra!

YOU CAN CALL ME
by J. Patrick Lewis

Polar Bear, but to others
I am known as
White Bear
Ice Bear
Sea Bear
Nanuk, the one who deserves great respect
The Ever-wandering One
Sailor of the Icebergs
White Sea Deer
Whale's Curse
Seal's Dread.
To the Ket people of Siberia,
I am *Grandfather.*
The Laplanders have named me
God's Dog or *Old Man in the Fur Coat.*
They say I am as smart as ten men
and as strong as twelve.

PUEDES LLAMARME
basado en "You Can Call Me"
por J. Patrick Lewis

Oso polar, pero para otros
soy conocido como
oso blanco,
oso del hielo,
oso del mar,
nanuk, el que merece gran respeto,
el que vaga siempre,
marinero de los icebergs,
venado blanco del mar,
amenaza de ballena,
temor de foca.
Para el pueblo queto, de Siberia,
soy *Abuelo.*
Los lapones me han dado el nombre
de *perro de Dios* o *anciano con abrigo de piel.*
Dicen que soy tan inteligente como diez hombres
y tan fuerte como doce.

HAPPY ADOPTION DAY
by Jane Yolen

This is the day we celebrate
Adoption Day, our family date,
The day that in that faraway year
I traveled from where I was to here.

By bus, by plane, by train, by car.
I carried my heart so very far
To find my place, to find my home,
The people I could call my own.

So on this day, let's all agree
To celebrate not only me,
But family.

FELIZ DÍA DE LA ADOPCIÓN
basado en "Happy Adoption Day"
por Jane Yolen

Este es el día que celebramos,
El día de la adopción, nuestra fecha familiar,
El día en que ese lejano año
Viajé de donde estaba hasta aquí.

Por autobús, por avión, por tren, por auto.
Llevé mi corazón tan tan lejos
Para encontrar mi lugar, para encontrar mi hogar,
Las personas a quien llamo mías.

Así que, en este día, acordemos celebrar
No solo yo,
Sino mi familia.

A LONG TIME AGO
by Jeannine Atkins

Some said, "Only a boy can become
a president, priest, artist, or spy.
Girls should keep quiet and still.
Stay out of the sea and the sky."

But strong women said, "Don't tell us *no*.
We'll speak up, swim deep, and explore.
Sports, science, and acting aren't just for men.
We can preach, paint, or prowl—and more."

In March, please cheer for women
who steer submarines or fly jets.
All together, let's follow new dreams.
The fight for fairness is not over yet!

HACE MUCHO TIEMPO
basado en "A Long Time Ago"
por Jeannine Atkins

Algunos decían que solo un hombre podía
ser presidente, sacerdote, artista o espía.
Las mujeres debían mantener silencio y tranquilidad,
fuera del cielo y del mar.

Pero ellas, fuertes, contestaron: "Un *no* no aceptamos.
Hablamos alto y claro, nadamos profundo y exploramos.
Los deportes, las ciencias, la actuación no son solo para hombres.
Podemos predicar, pintar, patrullar, que nadie se asombre".

En marzo, honren a las mujeres
que conducen submarinos o cohetes.
Juntos persigamos nuevos sueños.
¡La lucha por la justicia aún no ha terminado!

SINCERELY
by Robyn Hood Black

Dear Friend,

I see the thoughtful things you do.
Your words are always cheerful, too.

I noticed!
And I'm thanking you.

Sincerely,
Me

AFECTUOSAMENTE
basado en "Sincerely"
por Robyn Hood Black

Querido amigo:

Eres muy amable y atento,
y tus palabras son siempre de aliento.

¡Lo he advertido!
y te estoy agradecido.

Afectuosamente,
Yo

HAPPY BIRTHDAY, DR. SEUSS
by Carole Gerber

Thank you! Thank you! Dr. Seuss,
for setting that old *Lorax* loose.

For serving up *Green Eggs and Ham*
to grumpy, grumpy Sam-I-Am.

For *Horton's Who* and *Hop on Pop*.
Your silly verses do not stop!

Hooray for Diffendoofer Day!
keeps me laughing all the way.

Happy birthday on March two!
We love you, Dr. Seuss. We do!

FELIZ CUMPLEAÑOS, DR. SEUSS
basado en "Happy Birthday, Dr. Seuss"
por Carole Gerber

¡Gracias, gracias!, Dr. Seuss,
por soltar a ese viejo *Lorax*.

Por servir *Green Eggs and Ham*
al gruñón, gruñón Juan Ramón;

por *Horton's Who* y *Hop on Pop*.
¡Tus versos graciosos no tienen fin!

Hooray for Diffendoofer Day!
todo el tiempo me hace reír.

¡Feliz cumpleaños el dos de marzo!
Te amamos, Dr. Seuss, te amamos!

PICKY EATER
by Matt Forrest Esenwine

I love my Fruit Loops,
love my Kix,
love Cheerios
and even Trix.
I also like
my Apple Jacks—
but please don't give me
Sugar Smacks,
or stars or squares or flakes
you've found—
I only eat, you see,
what's *round*.

Note: cereal brand names are trademarks
owned by their companies

EXIGENTE PARA COMER
basado en "Picky Eater"
por Matt Forrest Esenwine

Me encantan mis Fruit Loops,
me encantan mis Kix,
me encantan los Cheerios
y hasta los Trix.
Y también me gustan
mis Apple Jacks—
pero, por favor
no me des Sugar Smacks,
ni estrellitas, ni cuadritos
ni copitos encontrados—
solo como
lo *redondo*.

Nota: los nombres de los cereales son marcas
registradas que pertenecen a sus empresas

DAYLIGHT SAVING TIME
by Shirley Duke

Spring forward!
It's Daylight Saving Time.
We change our clocks
Forward by one hour.
Five o'clock is now six.
We lose an hour of sleep but
We get to stay outside until late.

Fall back!
Daylight Saving Time ends today.
We change our clocks
Back by one hour.
Six o'clock becomes five.
We gain an hour of sleep today—hooray!
Darkness falls fast—but it's warm inside.

HORARIO DE VERANO
basado en "Daylight Saving Time"
por Shirley Duke

¡Adelante, primavera!
Comienza el horario de verano.
Adelantemos los relojes,
Como todos los años.
Las cinco serán las seis ahora.
Dormiremos menos,
Pero hasta más tarde jugaremos.

¡Vuelve el otoño!
Hoy termina el horario de verano.
Retrasemos los relojes,
Como todos los años.
Las seis serán las cinco ahora.
¡Hurra!, dormiremos más,
Cae la noche pronto, mas dentro hay calor.

FABLES
by Robert Schechter

Perhaps you know a story where
an animal is able
to talk the way a person talks?
It's possibly a fable.

If there's a moral at the end
then give the tale its label:
Don't call the tale a fairy tale
but call the tale a fable.

If pigs in pens and chicks in coops
and horses in their stable
can speak, and there's a lesson learned,
they must be in a fable.

FÁBULAS
basado en "Fables"
por Robert Schechter

¿Quizá conoces una historia
en la que un animal puede hablar
como hablan las personas?
Es posible que sea una fábula.

Si tiene moraleja al final,
dale a la historia su nombre:
no la llames cuento de hadas,
llámala fábula.

Si los cerdos del chiquero,
las gallinas del gallinero y los caballos del establo
hablan y te dan una enseñanza,
deben estar en una fábula.

ST. PATRICK'S DAY
by Esther Hershenhorn

March 17
the world turns green
to celebrate St. Patrick.
Green hats!
Green floats!
Green rivers, too!
March 17's green magic.

DÍA DE SAN PATRICIO
basado en "St. Patrick's Day"
por Esther Hershenhorn

El 17 de marzo,
el mundo se vuelve verde
para celebrar a San Patricio.
¡Sombreros verdes!
¡Carrozas verdes!
¡Ríos verdes también!
El 17 de marzo es magia verde.

SPRING

by Jane Lichtenberger Patton

At last . . . it's passed!
Not one more
wintry blast.

Warm breezes blow
(thanks to the sun),
and birds fly home
to nest with young.
The earth's in bloom,
new life's begun.
Spring's finally sprung . . . at last!

PRIMAVERA

basado en "Spring"
por Jane Lichtenberger Patton

Por fin . . . ¡ya pasó!
Se acabaron
las tormentas invernales.

Soplan cálidas brisas
(gracias al sol),
y regresan los pájaros
para anidar con sus pichones.
La tierra esta brotando,
nueva vida empezando.
¡Por fin floreció la primavera!

WORLD WATER DAY
by George Ella Lyon

See it flow: It's a river.
Stop it cold, and it's ice.
Watch it wave: It's the ocean
breaking once, breaking twice.

Water falls.
Water freezes.
Water mists,
and it pleases

oak and shark and butterfly
every thirsty thing that lives.
Next time you take a drink, think:
Life's the gift that water gives.

DÍA MUNDIAL DEL AGUA
basado en "World Water Day"
por George Ella Lyon

Mira cómo fluye: es un río.
En hielo se puede transformar.
Mira la ola: es el mar
que va y viene con gran brío.

Cae en rocío.
Cae en cascada.
Cae en forma de nevada,
y todo ser que está vivo,

pez o mariposa o roble,
calma su sed y se alivia.
Cuando bebas agua piensa
que el agua te regala la vida.

THE POETRY FRIDAY ANTHOLOGY FOR CELEBRATIONS

AT THE SEDER
by Buffy Silverman

My family gathers together,
the table is gleaming and bright.
We tell a great tale of our freedom—
a story for Passover night.

My brother slides under the table—
he's lurking beneath Grandpa's chair.
He's waiting to snatch the afikomen*
while Grandpa is leading a prayer.

My cousin has learned the four questions,
she blushes and sings them with pride:
Why are there matzos, salt water, and herbs?
Why must we lean to one side?

The answers are part of the story—
each year we recite it anew.
We remember a season of slavery,
we're thankful that season is through.

* The afikomen is a piece of matzo that's broken during the Seder and eaten at the end of the meal. In some families children steal the afikomen and ask for a reward for its return. In other families, an adult hides the afikomen and the child who finds it receives a prize.

EN EL SÉDER★
basado en "At the Seder" por Buffy Silverman

Mi familia se reúne,
la mesa brilla radiante.
Contamos el gran relato de nuestra libertad—
la historia para la noche de Pascua.

Mi hermano se mete bajo la mesa—
hasta la silla del abuelo,
espera el afikomán** con gran ilusión,
mientras el abuelo conduce la oración.

Mi prima supo las cuatro preguntas.
Se sonroja y las canta orgullosa:
¿Por qué el matzá, el agua salada y las hierbas?
¿Por qué nos inclinamos hacia un lado?

Las respuestas son parte de la historia—
la recitamos cada año de memoria.
Recordamos la esclavitud del pasado
y damos gracias: por fin ha terminado.

* Cena de Pascua.
** El afikomán es un trozo de matzá (pan ácimo) que se parte durante el Séder y se come al final de la cena. En algunas familias, los niños "roban" el afikomán y piden una recompensa para devolverlo. En otras familias, los adultos lo esconden y el niño que lo encuentra recibe un premio.

BREAK AN EGG
by Stephanie Hemphill

Papa challenges me to an egg fight.
I choose the one with a green stripe.

If your egg doesn't crack, then you win.
Is the flat or the pointy the strong end?

When our two eggs strike,
it sounds like broken ice.

My egg's smooth, not a scratch!
But Papa's egg begins to hatch.

Note: In cultures across the globe from India to Serbia to the Netherlands, there is a tradition of egg tapping contests. In my family, we hold an egg-boxing contest every Easter. When we dye eggs, everyone holds one aside for the match. and I'm not sure why, but the ugliest egg always seems to win.

ROMPE UN HUEVO
basado en "Break an Egg!"
por Stephanie Hemphill

Papá me desafía a una guerra de huevos.
Elijo uno con raya verde en el medio.

El huevo que no se parta será el ganador.
¿Es el extremo con punta o el redondo el mejor?

Cuando los huevos se choquen,
sonarán como el hielo que se rompe.

Mi huevo es suave, ¡y no se casca!
Pero el de papá comienza a salir del cascarón.

Nota: En muchas culturas, de la India a Serbia y a los Países Bajos, existe la tradición de hacer concursos de choque de huevos. En mi familia, siempre lo hacemos en Pascua. Cuando pintamos los huevos, todos reservamos uno para jugar, y, no sé por qué, parece que gana siempre el más feo.

BASEBALL'S OPENING DAY
by Shirley Duke

It's spring again!
It's time to play.
Brand new season—
today's the day.

The names are called.
Players run out.
Umps take the field.
The peanut guys shout.

The anthem is sung.
Now, the magic call.
It's time to start:
"Play ball!"

DÍA DE INAUGURACIÓN
DE LA TEMPORADA DE BÉISBOL
basado en "Baseball's Opening Day"
por Shirley Duke

¡La primavera llegó!
Empiecen ya las jugadas,
Que esta nueva temporada
Hoy por fin se inauguró.

Llaman a los equipos.
Salen los jugadores.
Se presentan los árbitros.
Gritan los vendedores.

Se canta el himno nacional.
Después, el mágico llamado
Del momento esperado:
"¡Empiecen a jugar!"

FIRST LAUGH, NAVAJO BABY
by Rose Ann Tahe and Nancy Bo Flood

Navajo baby,
Everyone is watching,
Waiting,
When will we hear your very first laugh?
Big brother, *Ninaai*, makes silly faces.
Nadi, big sister, tickles your toes with her fingers.
Mother, *Nima*, sings as she shows you the sunrise.
Grandmother, *Nimasani,* chants a corn pollen prayer.
So you will laugh—
Oh, baby, yes!
Awee' ch'ideeldlo'! Yaah!

Now we will celebrate,
With sweet cake and salt.
And welcome you,
Navajo baby,
Into our family,
Into your clans.

Note: The person who causes the baby to laugh wins the honor of hosting the "first laughter" celebration, with lots of family and lots of food—fry bread, mutton stew, and sweet "laughter" cake. The First Laugh Ceremony is the beginning of a Navajo child knowing "this is who I am and where I am from."

LA PRIMERA RISA DEL BEBÉ NAVAJO
basado en "First Laugh, Navajo Baby" por Rose Ann Tahe y Nancy Bo Flood

Bebé navajo,
todos observamos,
todos esperamos,
¿Cuándo oiremos tu primera risa?
Tu hermano mayor, *Ninaai*, hace muecas.
Nadi, tu hermana mayor, te hace cosquillas en los pies.
Tu mamá, *Nima*, canta mientras te muestra la salida del sol.
Tu abuela, *Nimasani,* entona una oración al polen de maíz.
Así te reirás
¡oh, bebé, sí!
¡Awee' ch'ideeldlo'! ¡Yaah!

Celebraremos ahora
con pasteles dulces y sal.
Bienvenido,
bebé navajo,
a nuestra familia,
a tu pueblo.

Nota: La persona que logra que el bebé se ría tiene el honor de ser anfitriona de la celebración de la Primera Risa, que se festeja con cantidad de familiares y de comida — pan frito, guiso de cordero y pastel "de la risa". La ceremonia de la Primera Risa es el momento en que el bebé empieza a saber quién es y de dónde proviene.

SOME REASONS
TO WRITE A POEM
by Bob Raczka

Because the cardinal on the snow-covered
branch is whistling

Because you bit into a hot pepper
by mistake

Because the moon changes shape

Because you woke up to the smell of bacon

Because your big toe stuck out through
the hole in your sock all day long

Because you wonder where passing trains
are coming from

or going to

ALGUNAS RAZONES
PARA ESCRIBIR UN POEMA
basado en "Some Reasons to Write a Poem"
por Bob Raczka

Porque el cardenal canta
sobre la nieve que cubre la rama

porque mordiste un chile picante
sin darte cuenta

porque la luna cambia de forma

porque el tocino te despertó con su aroma

porque el dedo gordo de tu pie se asoma
por el agujero del calcetín

porque te preguntas
de dónde vienen los trenes

o hacia dónde irán

TREE DAY CELEBRATION
by Ibtisam Barakat

In the city of Ramallah every April
we celebrate Tree Day . . .

Each child plants a sapling
and that brings everyone

closer to the land . . .

One year I chose a fig:
from day to day I measured
the size of its five-finger-shaped leaves

and like a school mate I stood next to it
and checked my height

I worried about it sleeping alone outside at night . . .
So I asked the moon to keep a ray of light
shining on it . . .

Every day after school I sat next to my fig tree
And told it stories that
only a person who has feet
And can walk and run can understand . . .

My tree silently told me the stories and secrets
only a being who has real roots
And can sit for a lifetime
Can share . . .

LA CELEBRACIÓN DEL DÍA DEL ÁRBOL
basado en "Tree Day Celebration" por Ibtisam Barakat

En la ciudad de Ramala celebramos
el día del árbol en abril.

Cada niño planta un retoño
y con ello nos acerca

más y más a la tierra.

Un año elegí una higuera
y día tras día medía
sus hojas, parecidas a una mano

Y como si fuera su compañero de escuela
me paraba a su lado y medía mi altura.

Preocupaba que durmiera sola afuera . . .
le pedí a la luna que dejara un rayo
encendido sobre ella.

A la vuelta de la escuela, me sentaba con mi higuera,
y le narraba historias
que solo una persona, con pies,
que corre y camina, puede comprender . . .

Mi árbol, en silencio, me contaba cuentos y secretos
de los que solo un ser con raíces de verdad,
siempre asentado en su lugar,
es capaz de compartir . . .

BOOKS
by Nancy White Carlstrom

Books are the best bridges
In all the world
Cross over
And you can be anyone
Anywhere
You can be me
I can be you
Together we can read
And meet each other halfway.

LOS LIBROS
basado en "Books"
por Nancy White Carlstrom

Los libros son los mejores puentes
En todo el mundo
Te invitan a ser alguien
De otro lugar
Cruza
Y tú puedes ser yo
Yo puedo ser tú
Si leemos juntos
Nos encontraremos a medio camino.

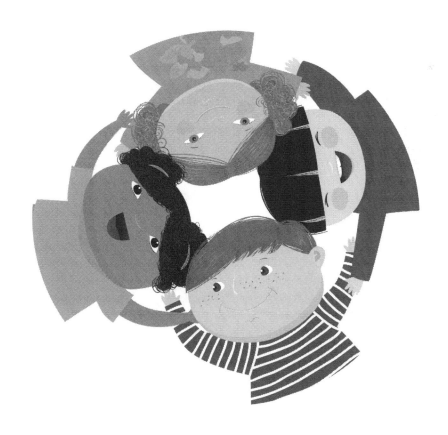

JUST WEIGHT!
(A CONVERSATION BETWEEN TWO HIPPOS)
by Heidi Bee Roemer

Harold thinks he's handsome.
Henry thinks he's hot.
But one thing they're both proud about
is that they weigh a lot.

Harold brags to Henry,
"I'm muscular, not fat.
I weigh more than you do, Dude.
I'm three *tons* to be exact!"

Henry is humungous.
Henry says, "Oh, please!
I'm heavier than you by far!"
But Harold disagrees.

Henry says. "I'll prove it.
Don't mean to spoil your fun,
but in *kilos* I'm two thousand,
seven hundred twenty-one!"

So the silly hippos argue
long into the night.
Their weight's the same--just different names!
Both of them are right!

Note: 2721.55 kilograms equals 3 tons.

2, 721 KILOS!

¡PROBLEMA DE PESO!
(CONVERSACIÓN ENTRE DOS HIPOPÓTAMOS)
basado en "Just Weight!
(A Conversation Between Two Hippos)"
por Heidi Bee Roemer

Harold piensa que es lindo.
Henry piensa que es atractivo.
Pero si de algo están orgullosos
es de su peso asombroso.

Harold presume con Henry,
"Amigo, tengo músculos, no soy gordo
y peso más que tú.
¡Tres *toneladas,* con exactitud!"

Henry es gigantesco
y le dice: "¡Por favor!
¡yo soy muchísimo más pesado!"
Pero no está de acuerdo Harold.

Henry dice: "Lo demostraré:
no quiero quitarte la ilusión,
¡pero en kilos peso dos mil
setecientos veintidós!"

Así los tontos hipopótamos
discuten hasta tarde.
El peso es el mismo ¡sólo el nombre cambió!
¡Los dos tienen razón!

Nota: 2721.55 kilogramos son 3 toneladas.

3 TONS!

I'M BIGGER
by Kristy Dempsey

You wobble.
I walk.
You babble.
I talk.
You sit
and drool
and swing,
while I draw
and dance
and sing.
I can say my ABCs.
You just jiggle
plastic keys.
I can run
and jump
and spin . . .
and when I do,
it makes you grin.
I am bigger.
You're so small.
(But I still love you
best of all.)

SOY MÁS GRANDE
basado en "I'm Bigger"
por Kristy Dempsey

Tú te tambaleas,
yo camino.
Tú balbuceas
cuando hablo contigo.
Sentado
y babeando,
oscilas a ambos lados,
mientras yo dibujo,
bailo
y canto.
Yo puedo decir el abecedario.
Tú solo sacudes
llaves de plástico.
Yo puedo correr
y saltar
y girar . . .
y cuando lo hago,
te hace sonreir.
Soy más grande.
Y tú, tan pequeño.
(Pero te quiero
más que a nadie.)

MY PLACE TO FLY
by Ted Scheu

The library
is where I go
to launch myself and fly.

I swoop and loop
above the earth
a thousand stories high.

MI LUGAR PARA VOLAR
basado en "My Place to Fly"
por Ted Scheu

La biblioteca
es el lugar donde voy
a lanzarme y volar.

Subo y bajo dando vueltas
por encima de la Tierra
trepado a miles de historias de alto.

STOP! LET'S READ
by Kristy Dempsey

Wherever you are,
it's time to stop!
Grab a book
and find a spot.
Look at pictures,
see new faces,
word by word,
discover places.
You say: *Read!*
and I'll join in.
Ready, set,
just begin . . .
Let's start slow
and pick up speed.
Hey, everyone!
It's time to read!

¡ALTO! A LEER
basado en "STOP! Let's Read!"
por Kristy Dempsey

Dondequiera que estés,
¡es momento de detenerte!
Toma un libro
y busca un sitio.
Mira las ilustraciones
ve caras nuevas,
palabra por palabra,
descubre lugares.
Tu di: ¡Lee!,
y me uniré.
Preparados, listos,
comencemos . . .
Empecemos despacio
y tomemos velocidad.
¡Oigan todos!
¡Es hora de leer!

POCKET CHANGE
by Kelly Ramsdell Fineman

The dime's the smallest, thinnest coin
made by the U.S. Mint.
It features Franklin Roosevelt,
a U.S. President.

The five-cent nickel's named after
the metal it comes from—
with Monticello on the back
and, on front, Jefferson.

The Lincoln penny's worth one cent;
one hundred make a buck.
Some people think if you find one,
you'll have a lot of luck.

George Washington, first President,
is every quarter's face.
Each quarter's back shows different things,
like monuments and states.

You might keep coins inside a bank,
in pockets, or a jar.
They tell you U.S. history
no matter where they are.

MONEDAS
basado en "Pocket Change"
por Kelly Ramsdell Fineman

La moneda de diez centavos es la más pequeña y delgada
que hace la Casa de la Moneda de los Estados Unidos.
En ella aparece el rostro Franklin Roosevelt,
un presidente del país.

La moneda de cinco centavos se fabrica con níquel
y en inglés lleva el nombre de este metal.
Se ve Monticello en la parte de atrás
y Jefferson en la de adelante.

La de un centavo tiene a Lincoln,
y con cien se forma un dólar.
Algunos creen que si encuentras una,
tendrás mucha fortuna.

George Washington, el primer presidente,
es la cara de la moneda de veinticinco centavos.
En el revés, cada una muestra cosas diferentes,
como monumentos o estados.

Puedes guardar monedas en un banco,
en los bolsillos o en un frasco.
Te cuentan la historia de los Estados Unidos
sin importar dónde las hayas reunido.

EARTH, YOU ARE
by Mary Lee Hahn

Earth, you are beautiful.
I love your flowers, blooming
in the vacant lot near the tracks.

Earth, you are funny.
The plunking acorns in my yard
are enough to make a new forest!

TIERRA, ERES
basado en "Earth, You Are"
por Mary Lee Hahn

Tierra, eres tan hermosa.
Me encantan las plantas que florecen
en los terrenos baldíos junto a las vías.

Tierra, eres graciosa.
¡Las bellotas de mi jardín
alcanzan para sembrar un bosque sin fin!

POCKET POEMS™ CARD
by Janet Wong

Memorizing
isn't hard

with your
Pocket Poems card.

Take a card out
when you eat.

Read out loud.
Again. Repeat.

Read. Bite.
Read. Chew.

Your poem will soon
be part of you!

TARJETA DE BOLSILLO
basado en "Pocket Poems™ Card"
por Janet Wong

Memorizar
es sencillo

con tu tarjeta
de bolsillo.

Toma una tarjeta
mientras comes.

Léela en voz alta.
Otra vez. Repítela.

Léela. Muerde.
Léela. Mastica.

¡El poema será parte de ti
enseguida!

EL BAILARÍN
por Jorge Argueta

Me encanta bailar
Cuando me pongo a bailar
Siento que la tierra
Me hace cosquillas en los pies

Soy un bailarín de acordeones
De trompetas
Maracas
Tambores y timbales

Soy un bailarín del viento
De la lluvia
De los pájaros
Soy un gusano, un trompo bailarín

Me gusta bailar a todas horas
Me encanta bailar salsa
Cumbia
Y también jazz

Si estoy durmiendo estoy bailando
Con mis sueños.

THE DANCER
by Jorge Argueta

I love dancing
When I start to dance
I feel as if the earth
tickles my feet

I am a dancer of accordions
trumpets
maracas
drums and timbales

I am a wind dancer
a rain dancer
a bird dancer
I am a worm, a top dancer

I like to dance at all times
I like to dance salsa
cumbia
and jazz too

If I am asleep, I am dancing
with my dreams.

CHILDREN'S DAY, BOOK DAY
by Pat Mora

Let's clap!
Say *día*, day,
Every day,
Kids and Books Day.

Let's tap.
Día, Day,
Every day,
Kids and Books Day.

Let's snap,
April fiestas,
Kids and books.
Happy days.

Clap, tap, snap.
Kids and books,
Every day.
Hooray!

EL DÍA DE LOS NIÑOS, EL DÍA DE LOS LIBROS
por Pat Mora

¡A aplaudir!
Digan *day,* día,
Cada día,
El día de los niños y los libros.

¡A zapatear!
Day, día,
Cada día,
El día de los niños y los libros.

¡A chasquear los dedos!
Las fiestas en abril,
Niños y libros.
¡Días felices!

¡A aplaudir! A zapatear! ¡A chasquear los dedos!
Niños y libros,
Cada día.
¡Viva!

WHAT WILL YOU CHOOSE, BABY?
by Linda Sue Park

Pen for writer.
Book for teacher.
Bowl of rice keeps hunger at bay.

Coins mean riches,
Thread, long life.
Cakes for the greedy—push them away!

Mama's laughter,
Daddy's camera.
Grandpa, Grandma, clap and cheer.

Hugs abounding.
Love surrounding.
Celebration! Your first year!

Note: On a Korean baby's first birthday, many families play "the
fortune game." Objects symbolizing various futures are placed in front
of the baby; whatever the baby chooses is said to predict its future.

BEBÉ, ¿QUÉ ELEGIRÁS?
basado en "What Will You Choose, Baby?" por Linda Sue Park

Un lapicero para el escritor.
Un libro para el maestro.
Una taza de arroz apaga el hambre.

Las monedas significan riqueza;
los hilos, larga vida.
Los pasteles para los egoístas: ¡recházalas!

La risa de mamá,
la cámara de papá.
Abuelito y abuelita, aplauden y animan.

Los abrazos abundan.
El amor rodea.
¡Celebración! ¡Tu primer año!

Nota: En el primer cumpleaños de un bebé coreano, muchas familias hacen el
"juego de la fortuna". Delante del bebé, se colocan objetos que simbolizan
distintos futuros; se dice que el objeto que elige el bebé predice su futuro.

I AM NOT A PLUCOT (BUT I KIND OF AM)
by Janet Wong

My father is Chinese.
He was born near Guangdong
and moved to San Francisco
when he was twelve years old.

My mother is Korean.
My father met her in Korea
when he was in the Army.
She came here as his wife.

Each kind of Asian is different, like
Italian is different from French,
Cuban is different from Mexican,
and apricots are not plums.

But sometimes you see plucots,
half-plum, half-apricot.
Grandma squeezes a plucot
and says, *Just like you!*

NO SOY UN PLUMCOT (PERO ALGO ASÍ)
basado en "I Am Not a Plucot (But I Kind of Am)" por Janet Wong

Mi padre es chino.
Nació cerca de Guangdong
y se mudó a San Francisco
cuando el tenía doce años.

Mi madre es coreana.
Mi padre la conoció en Corea,
cuando estaba en el Ejército,
y vino aqui como su esposa.

Cada asiático es distinto,
como son los italianos de los franceses,
los cubanos de los mexicanos
y los melocotones no son ciruelas.

Pero a veces se ven plumcots,
mitad ciruela, mitad albaricoque.
La abuelita exprime uno
y dice, *¡Igual que tú!*

SELFIE
by Lorie Ann Grover

Smile
Laugh
Click
Pic
See?
Me!

AUTOFOTO
basado en "Selfie"
por Lorie Ann Grover

Sonrisa
Risa
Clic
Foto
¿Ves?
¡Soy yo!

BICYCLE DREAMS
by Michael Salinger

my wheels are spinning
pedals are turning
hands on the handlebars
as I roll along
training wheels gone
a bike riding superstar
my thumb rings the bell
as I speed down the block
wind whooshes through my hair
I love riding my bike
'cause it makes me feel
like I can go anywhere

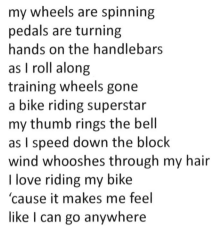

Note: Unlike driving a car or riding a bus, pedaling a bicycle makes the rider both the engine and the driver. It's the closest we can come to self-powered flying!

SUEÑOS DE BICICLETA
basado en "Bicycle Dreams"
por Michael Salinger

mis ruedas dan vueltas
los pedales giran con fuerza
sostengo el manubrio sin tregua
y voy rodando
sin las rueditas de entrenamiento
y soy un superciclista
la campanilla suena que suena
mientras acelero por la vereda
y el viento zumba en mi cabellera
me encanta manejar mi bicicleta
porque con ella declaro
que puedo ir a todos lados

Nota: A diferencia de lo que sucede con autos o los autobuses, quien maneja una bicicleta es, a la vez, motor y conductor. ¡Es lo más parecido a volar por nuestros propios medios!

LET'S GO
by Merry Bradshaw

Stretch High
Stretch Wide
Jump Forward
Jump Back

Lean Left
Lean Right
Hop Once
Hop Twice

Reach Up
Reach Down
Twist Small
Twist Tall

Shake Fast
Shake Slow
Touch Nose
Touch Toes

Stand Up
Let's Go!

VAMOS
basado en "Let's Go"
por Merry Bradshaw

Estírate
Ensánchate
Salta hacia adelante
Salta hacia atrás

Inclínate a la izquierda
Inclínate a la derecha
Brinca una vez
Brinca dos

Hacia arriba al cielo
Hacia abajo al suelo
Gira de costado
Gira al otro lado

Sacúdete rápido
Y también despacio
Tócate la nariz sin mirar
Y los zapatos sin vacilar

Párate
¡Vamos!

PET WEEK SHOW-AND-TELL

by Eric Ode

Pet Week! Pet Week!
Frogs croak, mice squeak.
Rabbits hop, snakes hiss.
Crickets chirp, fish kiss.

Dogs howl, horses neigh.
Turtles crawl, kittens play.
Lizards scurry, parrots speak.
Hurry! Hurry! Pet Week!

PRESENTACIÓN DE LA SEMANA DE LAS MASCOTAS

basado en "Pet Week Show-and-Tell" por Eric Ode

¡La Semana de las Mascotas se avecina!
Las ranas croan, los ratones chillan.
Saltan los conejos, sisean las serpientes.
Grillan los grillos, los peces besan sonrientes.

Ladridos de perros, relinchos de caballos.
Tortugas, muy lentas; gatitos, jugando.
Los lagartos huyen, los loros dicen rimas.
¡La Semana de las Mascotas se avecina!

A TEACHER KNOWS
by Eric Ode

A teacher knows
why sparrows sing,
why dolphins swim
and hornets sting,
why trees are green
and dirt is brown,
why clouds stay up
and rain falls down.

A teacher knows
why honey's sweet
and why the chickens
cross the street.
But how a student
learns and grows
is also what
a teacher knows.

UN MAESTRO SABE
basado en "A Teacher Knows"
por Eric Ode

Un maestro sabe
por qué cantan los gorriones,
por qué nadan los delfines
y pican los avispones;
por qué los árboles son verdes
y la tierra es café;
por qué hay nubes en lo alto
y la lluvia cae hacia abajo.

Un maestro sabe
por qué la miel es dulce
y por qué las gallinas
cruzan la calle.
Y cómo aprende y crece
un estudiante
es también algo
que un maestro sabe.

LAUGHING
by Cynthia Grady

Whenever Gran begins to laugh,
    her shoulders shake,
    her arms jiggle,
    her eyes close,
    her mouth opens.
At last, we hear a giggle.

LA RISA
basado en "Laughing"
por Cynthia Grady

Cuando la abu está por reír,
    sacude los hombros,
    mueve los brazos,
    cierra los ojos,
    abre la boca;
y su risa, por fin, explota.

LOOK FOR THE HELPERS
by Michelle Heidenrich Barnes

Look for the helpers
The healers
The givers

The arms-open
Hand-holding
Everyday heroes

The ones who bring food
Extra clothes
And first aid

Who offer safe shelter
A roof
And a bed

Follow their lead
Be a hugger
A helper

A friend who will listen
A person
Who cares

BUSCA A LOS AYUDANTES
basado en "Look for the Helpers"
por Michelle Heidenrich Barnes

Busca a los ayudantes
Los que curan
Los donantes

Los brazos abiertos
Las manos tendidas
Héroes todos los días

Los que brindan alimentos
Prendas y abrigos
Y primeros auxilios

Ofrecen refugio
Cama, techo
Y cobijo

Sigue su camino
Sé un buen amigo
Alguien que ayuda

Un amigo que escucha
Y acompaña
Y se preocupa

TREASURE HUNT
by Sandy Asher

I wonder . . .
who invented glass?
how come haircuts don't hurt?
where does the wind start?
I wonder . . .

I search . . .
library shelves,
books,
pages,
pictures.
Looking for answers,
I dig deep . . .

BÚSQUEDA DEL TESORO
basado en "Treasure Hunt"
por Sandy Asher

Me pregunto . . .
¿quién inventó el vidrio?
¿por qué un corte de cabello no te va a lastimar?
el viento, ¿de dónde vendrá?
Me pregunto . . .

Busco . . .
en la biblioteca,
libros,
páginas,
fotos.
Buscando respuestas
escarbo hondo . . .

MOM'S PERFUME
by Janet Wong

Mom's perfume
is like a temporary tattoo
you can wash off—

that gets pressed back
into my skin
every time she hugs me.

EL PERFUME DE MAMÁ
basado en "Mom's Perfume"
por Janet Wong

El perfume de mamá
es como un tatuaje temporal
que se puede lavar—

se me pega
en la piel
cada vez que me abraza.

THINGS NOT TO DO
by Eileen Spinelli

Don't pick your nose.
Don't push in line.
Don't grab for things.
Don't stomp. Don't whine.

Don't slurp your soup.
Don't burp. And please
don't sneeze into
your sister's peas.

Don't say mean things.
Don't lie. Don't litter.
Don't hide to scare
the babysitter.

Don't grumble when
you're doing chores.
Don't mumble words.
And don't slam doors.

And while you're at it
don't forget—
life's nicer with
good etiquette.

COSAS QUE NO SE HACEN
basado en "Things Not to Do"
por Eileen Spinelli

No te escarbes la nariz.
No empujes en la fila.
No arrebates las cosas.
No atropelles. No lloriquees.

No sorbas la sopa.
No eructes. Y no estornudes,
por favor, en los chícharos
de tu hermana.

No digas cosas malas.
No mientas. En la calle, no tires basura.
No te escondas para asustar
a la niñera.

No te quejes
cuando haces las tareas.
No hables entre dientes.
Y no azotes las puertas.

Y, de paso,
no te olvides:
la vida es linda
con buenos modales.

A DREAM WITHOUT HUNGER
by Michael J. Rosen

Imagine the day—how else
can change begin?—when no one

goes to bed hungry
and no one rises hungry.

Imagine that dawn
when all of us awaken

from hunger's nightmare
and breakfast is no dream.

Imagine such a day.
It can't be far away.

UN SUEÑO SIN HAMBRE
basado en "A Dream Without Hunger"
por Michael J. Rosen

Imagina el día—así
comienza el cambio—en que nadie

se acuesta con hambre
y nadie se levanta con hambre.

Imagina ese amanecer
en que todos nos despertemos

de la pesadilla del hambre
y el desayuno no sea un sueño.

Imagina un día así.
No puede estar muy lejos.

RECIPE FOR A TWIN BIRTHDAY
by Renée M. LaTulippe

Double the cake
double the names
double the ice cream
double the games
double the kids
double the noise
and don't forget
to double the toys!

RECETA PARA UN CUMPLEAÑOS DE MELLIZOS
basado en "Recipe for a Twin Birthday"
por Renée M. LaTulippe

Duplica el pastel,
duplica los nombres,
duplica el helado,
duplica los juegos,
duplica los niños,
duplica el ruido
y no olvides
¡duplicar los juguetes!

MY GRADUATION
by JoAnn Early Macken

Here's my graduation picture.
See our caps and gowns?
We felt like queens and kings in robes
with tassels on our crowns.

I waited for my turn to march
when Teacher called my name.
She shook my hand and gave me
a diploma in a frame.

Douglas tripped and ripped his gown.
Rachel lost her cap.
We ate some cake. We said goodbye.
We all went home to nap.

MI GRADUACIÓN
basado en "My Graduation"
por JoAnn Early Macken

Esta es la foto de mi graduación.
¿Ves nuestros birretes y togas?
Nos sentimos reinas y reyes con batas
y borlas en la corona.

Esperé mi turno y pasé
cuando la maestra dijo mi nombre.
Me dio la mano y me entregó
en un marco el diploma.

Douglas tropezó, y la toga se le rompió.
Rachel perdió su birrete.
Comimos pastel. Nos dijimos adios.
Y fuimos a casa a tomar la siesta.

CAMPING
by Joy Acey

One hundred mosquitoes,
two dogs,
three owls,
four frogs
have all gathered by
my tent to croon—
singing a song to the full moon.
I hear a buzzing,
howling, hooting,
croaking-cheep!
It is so noisy
I cannot sleep.

CAMPAMENTO
basado en "Camping"
por Joy Acey

Cien mosquitos,
dos perritos,
tres lechuzas,
cuatro ranas
en mi carpa cantan
y en su voz resuena
una melodía a la luna llena.
¡Los oigo zumbando,
ladrando, ululando
y croando!
Con tanto alboroto,
no puedo dormir.

A MARCHING BAND OF VITAMINS
by Michele Krueger

let's celebrate potatoes
baked and mashed and fried,
let's toot the horn for yellow corn,
wave lettuce leaves with pride

a parade of red tomatoes
and bright green grapes in bunches,
will fill our hungry bellies
at recesses and lunches

let's bang the drum for broccoli,
for crunchy carrot sticks,
for pumpkin pie and purple plums
and berries we can pick

a marching band of vitamins
in every single bite,
a month of fruits and vegetables
for everyone's delight!

UNA BANDA DE VITAMINAS
basado en "A Marching Band of Vitamins"
por Michele Krueger

Celebremos por las papas
horneadas, en puré y fritas;
toquemos la trompeta por el maíz amarillo,
agitemos con orgullo las hojas de lechuga.

Un desfile de tomates rojos
y uvas verdes en racimo
nos llenarán la panza cuando tiene hambre
en recreos y almuerzos.

Toquemos el tambor por el brócoli,
por los crujientes bastones de zanahoria,
por el pie de calabaza y las ciruelas moradas
y las bayas recolectadas.

Una banda de vitaminas
en cada bocado,
un mes de frutas y vegetales
¡para delicia de chicos y grandes!

JACKSON

by Libby Martinez

I once knew a swan
named Jackson,
with feathers
white as the moon,
and a neck
long and black as night,
shaped like the letter S.

Some people think
animals are just animals
because they cannot speak,
but I knew Jackson,
and Jackson knew me,
even though we never
said a word.

Note: Poet Libby Martinez was once the Director of School & Community Partnerships for the Philadelphia Zoo, the oldest zoo in America. Jackson, a black-necked swan, lived at the zoo.

JACKSON

basado en "Jackson" por Libby Martinez

Conocí una vez a un cisne
llamado Jackson,
tenía las plumas
blancas como la luna
y un larguísimo cuello
con forma de *S*
negro como la noche.

A pesar de los que piensen
que los animales no sienten
porque no pueden hablar,
yo conocí a Jackson,
y Jackson me conoció a mí,
y, sin decir una palabra,
nos supimos comunicar.

Nota: Antes de ser escritora de libros infantiles, Libby Martinez fue Directora de Asociaciones Escolares y Comunitarias para el Zoológico de Philadelphia, el más antiguo de los Estados Unidos. Jackson era un cisne de cuello negro que vivía en el zoológico.

OH SUMMER BOOKS
(to the tune of "O Tannenbaum")
by Diana Murray

Oh summer books, oh summer books,
I love to turn your pages.
I find you at the library—
the coolest summer place to be!
Oh summer books, oh summer books,
I love to turn your pages.

LIBROS DE VERANO
(con la melodía de "Árbol de Navidad")
basado en "Oh Summer Books"
por Diana Murray

Libros, libros de verano,
me encanta pasar tus paginas.
Los encontre en la biblioteca –
¡lugar mas suave del calido verano!
Libros, libros de verano,
me encanta pasar tus paginas.

YO-YO
by George Ella Lyon

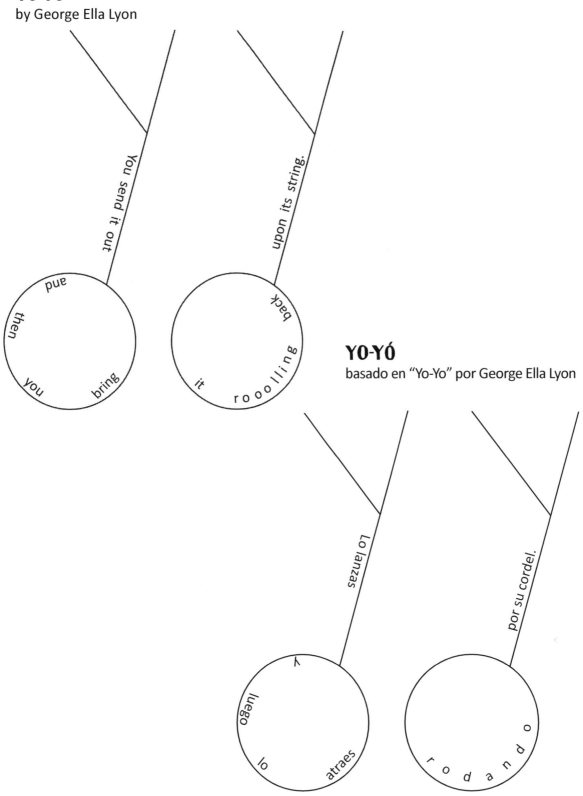

YO-YÓ
basado en "Yo-Yo" por George Ella Lyon

RED, WHITE, AND BLUE
by Libby Martinez

My favorite colors
are red, white, and blue,
the colors of the flag
that flaps,
and snaps,
and waves in the wind,
in front of my *abuelo's* house.

Sometimes we stand
in the cool green grass,
put our hand
over our heart,
look up at the flag
and count the fifty stars
for all fifty states.

My *abuelo* says,
"This flag belongs to everyone
who loves this country,
América,
because this country
loves each of us."

ROJO, BLANCO Y AZUL
basado en "Red, White, and Blue"
por Libby Martinez

Mis colores preferidos
son el rojo, el blanco y el azul,
colores de la bandera
que flamea,
se sacude
y con el viento ondea
frente a la casa de mi abuelo.

A veces nos paramos
en el césped fresco,
nos ponemos
la mano sobre el corazón,
miramos la bandera
y contamos las cincuenta estrellas,
una por cada estado.

El abuelo me explica:
"Esta es la bandera
de quienes aman a este país,
los Estados Unidos de América,
porque este país nos ama
a cada uno de nosotros".

A DAY TO HONOR FATHERS
by Carole Gerber

Papá, Vader, Babbo, Tad.
Babba, Otac, Apa, Dad.

Tatti, Tata, Tevs, and *Appa.*
Pita-ji, Daidí, Isa, Bapa.

Around the world, we children say,
Thank you! Happy Father's Day!

Note:

papá: Spanish
vader: Dutch
babbo: Italian
tad: Welsh
babba: Arabic
otac: Croatian, Bosnian
apa: Hungarian
dad: English
tatti: Yiddish
tata: Romanian
tevs: Latvian
appa: Korean
pita-ji: Hindi
daidí: Irish
isa: Estonian
bapa: Indonesian

UN DÍA PARA HONRAR A LOS PADRES
basado en "A Day to Honor Fathers"
por Carole Gerber

Papá, *vader, babbo, tad.*
babba, otac, apa, dad.

Tatti, tata, tevs y *appa.*
Pita-ji, daidí, isa, bapa.

En todo el mundo, los niños dicen,
¡Gracias! ¡Feliz Día del Padre!

Nota:

papá: español
vader: neerlandés
babbo: italiano
tad: galés
babba: árabe
otac: croata, bosnio
apa: húngaro
dad: inglés
tatti: yidis
tata: rumano
tevs: letón
appa: coreano
pita-ji: hindi
daidí: irlandés
isa: estonio
bapa: indonesio

CAR, BUS, TRAIN, OR BIKE
by Juanita Havill

Grandma's coming to visit me.
How will she travel? Let me see.

Drive her car. It's not far.
Hop on the bus. A stop's near us.
Take the train—in sun or rain.
Ride her bike. What's not to like?

None of the above today.
Grandma's walking all the way.

AUTO, AUTOBÚS, TREN O BICI
basado en "Car, Bus, Train, or Bike"
por Juanita Havill

Mi abuelita vendrá a visitarme.
¿De qué manera hará el viaje?

Vendrá en auto, no es muy lejos.
Subirá al autobús. Hay una parada cerca.
Tomará el tren, bajo la lluvia o el sol.
Vendrá en bici, ¿Por qué no?

Parece que no acerté:
¡mi abuelita vino a pie!

JUNETEENTH
by Charles Waters

On June 19th
We escaped
Our shackles of darkness
For the daylight of freedom
Amen.

Note: Juneteenth is a nationwide celebration
recognizing the termination of slavery
on June 19, 1865.

JUNETEENTH
basado en "Juneteenth"
por Charles Waters

El 19 de junio
Rompimos
Las cadenas de la oscuridad
Para iluminarnos con la luz de la libertad
Amén.

Nota: *Juneteenth* es la celebración nacional
que reconoce el 19 de junio de 1865 como
el fin de la esclavitud.

SUMMER IN ALASKA
by Nancy White Carlstrom

Baseball at midnight without lights.
A sky too bright for stars.
The garden growing giant cabbages.
The mosquitoes whining their long summer song.
Running, playing, staying up till late   late   late.
And my mama says, "Wait!
You better remember this.
So you can put it on like a warm snug coat
And wear it when winter comes."

Note: For 18 years I lived with my family in Fairbanks, Alaska where we stored up light from the midnight sun for our long winter's darkness.

VERANO EN ALASKA
basado en "Summer in Alaska"
por Nancy White Carlstrom

Béisbol a medianoche sin luz artificial.
El cielo no está oscuro: está el brillo solar.
En la huerta crecen repollos gigantes.
Los mosquitos zumban su larga canción veranal.
Corremos, saltamos, no nos acostamos hasta muy muy tarde.
Y mamá aconseja, "¡Tranquilos, aguarden!
Graben esto en la memoria
Como consuelo y abrigo
Para cuando venga el frío".

Nota: Viví con mi familia durante dieciocho años en Fairbanks, Alaska, donde guardábamos luz del sol de medianoche para la prolongada oscuridad del invierno.

HAPPY PRIDE!
by Lesléa Newman

My two moms take me by the hand
to stand behind the marching band.
The music plays, we clap and march
beneath the rainbow-colored arch.
Our friends and neighbors smile and cheer—
Hip Hip Hooray! Gay Pride is here!

¡FELIZ DÍA DEL ORGULLO!
basado en "Happy Pride!"
por Lesléa Newman

Mis dos mamás me llevan de la mano,
hasta pararnos detrás de la banda.
Suena la música, aplaudimos y marchamos
bajo el inmenso arco iris.
Nuestros amigos y vecinos aplauden a nuestro paso—
¡felices porque el orgullo gay ha llegado!

WISHES AROUND THE WORLD
by Andrea Cheng

We stretch the dough
until it is taller than me!
Long noodles for a long life,
Grandma Nai Nai says.

While the noodles cook,
I help Mommika Granny
stack the layers
of my birthday cake:
chocolate cream,
sponge cake,
chocolate cream,
sponge cake
with caramel on top.

In red icing,
my grandmas write
Happy Birthday!
in Chinese and Hungarian.
I add the English
by myself.

After lunch,
I blow out my candles
with a breath so strong
that my good wishes
will fly
around the world.

DESEOS POR TODO EL MUNDO
basado en "Wishes Around the World"
por Andrea Cheng

Estiramos la masa
¡hasta que es más alta que yo!
Fideos largos para una larga vida,
dice la abuelita Nai Nai.

Mientras los fideos se cocinan,
ayudo a la abuelita Mommika
a apilar las capas
de mi pastel de cumpleaños:
crema de chocolate,
bizcocho esponjoso,
crema de chocolate,
bizcocho esponjoso
con caramelo encima.

Con glasé rojo,
mis abuelas escriben
¡Feliz Cumpleaños!
en chino y en húngaro.
Yo solita lo agrego
en inglés.

Después de almorzar,
soplo las velitas
con tanta tanta fuerza
que mis buenos deseos
volarán
por todo el mundo.

"BREAK-FAST" AT NIGHT
by Ibtisam Barakat

In the Muslim month of Ramadan
Muslims fast from morning to evening . . .

They break the fast and eat
only after sunset . . .

Do you now know
What the word "breakfast" means?

During the day of fasting,
people look at their watches often

They count the hours and the minutes
until it is time to taste the feast . . .

Do you know that feeling
of waiting for a treat?

Many children who are five
stand on their toes to look old enough to fast.

But they are told:
not until you grow stronger . . .

From refusing to eat even chewing gum
I have learned that every bite of food is a present

and to get up every morning and
have breakfast is a daily celebration . . .

After Ramadan one becomes thin
like the new moon

but one is filled with light that
will be growing . . .

"DES-AYUNO" POR LA NOCHE
basado en "'Break-Fast' at Night"por Ibtisam Barakat

En su mes de Ramadán, los musulmanes
ayunan desde la mañana hasta la tarde . . .

Rompen el ayuno y comen
solo después de que el sol se pone . . .

¿Entiendes ahora el significado
de la palabra *desayuno*?

Durante el día de ayuno,
todos miran su reloj a menudo.

Cuentan las horas y los minutos que faltan
para saborear el festín . . .

¿Conoces esa sensación
de esperar algo delicioso?

Muchos niños de cinco años se paran en puntas de pie
para parecer más grandes, así pueden ayunar.

Pero les dicen que no pueden
hasta que sean más fuertes . . .

Rehusando comer hasta goma de mascar
he aprendido que cada bocado es un regalo

y que levantarse por la mañana
y tomar el desayuno es una celebración diaria . . .

Después de Ramadán uno queda delgado
como la luna nueva,

pero repleto de una luz
que seguirá creciendo . . .

PICNIC CHANT
by Laura Purdie Salas

Picnic
basket.
What's
inside?
Crispy
chicken,
golden,
fried!

Apples,
cookies,
crunchy
chips,
march
like
ants
right
to
my
lips!

CANCIÓN DEL PICNIC
basado en "Picnic Chant"
por Laura Purdie Salas

Canasta
de *picnic*.
¿Qué hay
dentro?
Pollo
frito
¡dorado,
crujiente!

Manzanas,
galletas,
papalinas
crocantes
¡marchan
como
hormigas
derecho
a
mi
boca!

ON HALFWAY DAY
by Janet Wong

We each had half a sandwich
then we waited half an hour—
so the food could sink
halfway to our feet.

Then we halfway-ran
to the neighborhood pool,
three whole blocks,
at the end of the street.

We shook off our shoes
and set down our towels.
My sister made sure
my suit was on right.

We swam until dinner—
half a dog and half a burger—
then we watched half a movie
and we said good night!

EN LA MITAD DEL AÑO
basado en "On Halfway Day"
por Janet Wong

Comimos medio sándwich,
esperamos media hora
a que la comida medio
nos bajeba a los pies.

Luego medio corrimos
a la alberca del barrio,
tres cuadras enteras,
donde topa la calle.

Nos quitamos los tenis
y tiramos las toallas.
Mi hermana checó
mi traje de baño.

Nadamos hasta la cena—
medio *hot dog* y hamburguesa,
luego vimos media película
¡y nos dijimos buenas noches!

INDEPENDENCE DAY
by Linda Dryfhout

Country's freedom.
Red, white, blue.
Parades, picnics,
barbecue.

Friends and family,
yummy food.
Sharing good times,
gratitude.

Fireworks popping,
look up high.
Pinwheels of color
light the sky.

Let's celebrate Fourth of July!

DÍA DE LA INDEPENDENCIA
basado en "Independence Day"
por Linda Dryfhout

Libertad del país,
rojo, blanco y azul.
Desfiles, *picnics*,
parrilladas.

Amigos y familiares,
comida deliciosa.
Buenos momentos
y gratitud.

Cohetes estallando,
mira en lo alto.
Molinetes de colores
alumbran el cielo.

¡Celebremos el 4 de Julio!

LET THE GAMES BEGIN
by Rebecca Kai Dotlich

It's okay to play
all day
loooooong!
You have an excuse, you do!

Imagine—Imagine.
24/7.
A universe of fun.
A slice of game Heaven.

POW.
BLAST.
Cosmic moons.
Step into a world
of mad cartoons.
Towers of bricks—
build and knock down.
Discover a wild
and wacky town.

Swap powers with heroes,
in a world long gone . . .

it's a Video Game Day
marathon!

QUE COMIENCEN LOS JUEGOS
basado en "Let the Games Begin"
por Rebecca Kai Dotlich

¡Está bien jugar
tooooooodo el día
sin parar!
Ya tienes una excusa, ¡hazlo!

Imagina—Imagina
24/7.
Un universo de diversión,
un trocito del paraíso de juegos.

EXPLOSIÓN.
¡BOM!
Lunas galácticas.
Entras en un mundo
de historietas fantásticas.
Torres de ladrillos,
construidas y destruidas.
Descubres una ciudad
loca y de maravilla.

Intercambias poderes con los héroes
en un mundo que ya desapareció . . .

¡Es un maratón
del Día de Videojuegos!

A PAPER BAG IS NEVER EMPTY
by Laura Purdie Salas

Even when empty,
a bag's always packed.
It's full of ideas—
bazillions, in fact!

Puppets and silly hats,
fringed vests and flags
are just a few things
packed inside empty bags.

UNA BOLSA DE PAPEL NUNCA ESTÁ VACÍA
basado en "A Paper Bag Is Never Empty"
por Laura Purdie Salas

Aun cuando esté vacía,
una bolsa está siempre llena:
repleta de ideas,
¡montonales, en realidad!

Títeres, gorros chistosos,
chalecos con flecos, banderas . . .
son solo algunas cosas que podrían
guardarse en bolsas vacías.

OBON
by Holly Thompson

we dress in *yukata*—
Mama, Papa, Baba, Jiji,
little Kenji and me
and walk to the schoolyard
all lit up with lanterns

friends and families
neighbors and shopkeepers
all wait for the music
and Baba takes my hand
as the crowd grows

when the songs start
a drum goes *DON DON donDON*
but I'm shy to join the dance
till Baba says *watch me*
and I follow, copying her

everyone joins, the circle grows
step forward, step back
hands high, hands low
our whole village together
our whole village a circle

to welcome spirits home

Note: In Japan, Obon is a festival celebrated in July or August. Obon is a time when the spirits of ancestors are believed to visit. Bonfires, special foods, and Obon dancing—known as bon-odori—welcome the spirits home. At the end of the three days of Obon, floating lanterns and sending-off fires guide the spirits back to their spirit world.

OBON
basado en "Obon" por Holly Thompson

nos vestimos con *yukata*—
Mamá, Papá, Baba, Jiji,
el pequeño Kenji y yo
y vamos al patio de la escuela
a la luz de farolitos

amigos y familiares
vecinos y tenderos
esperan la música
y Baba toma mi mano
cuando la multitud aumenta

al empezar las canciones
el tambor suena *DON DON don DON*
pero a mi bailar me da vergüenza
hasta que Baba dice *mírame a mí*
y copio lo que hace ella

todos se reúnen, se agranda el círculo
un paso adelante, un paso atrás
manos arriba, manos abajo
está reunida toda nuestra aldea
toda nuestra aldea en un círculo

para recibir a los espíritus

Nota: Obon es una fiesta de tres días que se celebra en Japón en julio o agosto. Según la creencia, es el momento en que regresa el espíritu de los antepasados. Para recibirlos, se hacen fogatas, comidas especiales y danzas —llamadas *bon-odori*. Al final de los festejos, farolitos flotantes y fogatas guían a los espíritus de regreso a su mundo.

BOATS
by Sara Holbrook

I celebrate
what sails
and floats,
from ships at sea
to fishing boats.
In bathtubs, lakes
and river flows,
on puddles,
ponds and undertows.
I hope my little bobbing boat
will ride the waves,
through highs and lows,
and rising,
dropping,
stay afloat.

BOTES
basado en "Boats" por Sara Holbrook

Celebro todo
lo que navega
y flota,
desde barcos en el mar
hasta barcas de pescar.
En tinas, en lagos
en ríos, en charcos,
en estanques, en corrientes de resaca.
Espero que mi barquito se hamaque
cabalgue sobre las olas,
desde arriba, hacia abajo,
y subiendo
y bajando,
se mantenga flotando.

MOON WALK—
JULY 21, 1969
by Susan Blackaby

Neil Armstrong
landed the Eagle
in a tranquil sea.
Then he stepped out to:

Moon walk hop.
Moon walk tromp.
Moon plod, spring, jump,
stride, bounce, leap.

He left moon walk tracks
and moon walk traces—
the first footsteps across
the face of the Man in the Moon.

CAMINATA LUNAR—
21 DE JULIO DE 1969
basado en "Moon Walk—July 21, 1969"
por Susan Blackaby

Neil Armstrong
con el Águila alunizó
en un tranquilo mar.
Salió de la nave y dio

un salto lunar,
una caminata lunar,
un salto lento, largo, lunar,
zancadas, rebotes, brincotes.

Allí dejó rastros de la caminata lunar
señales y marcas:
las primeras huellas
del Hombre en la Luna.

NATIONAL HAMMOCK DAY
by Douglas Florian

Today is National Hammock Day:
One of my favorite days.
No need to worry or to fret—
I just relax and laze.
Upon my hammock I will swing,
Beneath the shade of trees.
Too bad I'm in Alaska and
It's minus five degrees.

DÍA NACIONAL DE LA HAMACA
basado en "National Hammock Day"
por Douglas Florian

Hoy es el Día Nacional de la Hamaca:
Uno de los que me gustan más.
No me preocupo por nada,
Solo descanso y holgazaneo.
Sobre la hamaca me balanceo,
Bajo la sombra de los árboles.
Lástima que estoy en Alaska
Y hay cinco grados bajo cero.

I SCREAM!
by Lee Wardlaw

I want to
S C R E A M
for ice cream!
My favorite frozen treat.
Its nippy, lick-y richness
is smooth
and chilling-sweet.

I want to
S C R E A M
for ice cream!
But instead,
I'll have to hum.
My dessert is just so frosty
id bade by tung go nub!

¡GRITO!
basado en "I Scream!"
por Lee Wardlaw

¡Quiero
G R I T A R
por el helado!
Mi golosina congelada preferida.
Cada exquisita lengüetada fría
es una suave dulzura
refrescante.

¡Quiero
G R I T A R
por el helado!
Pero, en cambio,
tendré que tararear.
Mi postre está tan congelado
¡que mi engua etá paalizada!

HOW TO MAKE A FRIEND
by Jane Heitman Healy

You start by saying *Hi there,*
Hello, Aloha, Ciao—
If someone answers back to you,
Smile and nod and bow.

You might try saying *Hola,*
Salut, Goddag, Shalom.
If someone answers back to you,
They might be far from home.

A friend begins by greeting
Those they meet along the way
To make them feel welcome
At home, at school, at play.

CÓMO HACERSE DE UN AMIGO
basado en "How to Make a Friend"
por Jane Heitman Healy

Comienzas diciendo *¿Como está?*
Hola, Aloha, Ciao—
Si alguien te responde,
sonríe, saluda con la cabeza e inclínate.

Puedes intentar decir *Hello,*
Salut, Goddag, Shalom.
Si alguien te responde,
debe de estar lejos de casa.

La amistad comienza saludando
a los que encuentras en el camino
para que se sientan bienvenidos
en tu casa, en la escuela, en los juegos.

TODAY'S THE DAY!
by Lee Wardlaw

Up early.
Family flurry.

Bake a cake.
Decorate.

Guests arrive.
Come inside!

Brand new clothes.
Let's pose.

Sneak a lick.
Cameras click.

Birthday song.
Sing along.

Candle glow.
Ready . . . BLOW!

Lots of toys.
Lots of noise!

What fun.
Birthday's done.

But another year
has just begun!

¡HOY ES EL DÍA!
basado en "Today's the Day!"
por Lee Wardlaw

Arriba temprano.
Alboroto familiar.

Hornear un pastel.
Decorar.

Llegan los invitados.
¡Entren!

Ropa nueva.
Posemos.

Sacamos la lengua.
Cámaras, clic.

Canción de cumpleaños.
Cantamos.

Velitas encendidas.
Listos . . . ¡SOPLA!

Montones de juguetes.
¡Mucho ruido!

¡Qué divertido!
Cumpleaños terminado.

¡Pero otro año
apenas ha comenzado!

FAMILY DAY
by Francisco X. Alarcón

we spend Sunday
at our grandparents'
home together

with uncles and aunts
lots of little cousins
relatives and friends

while us children
get to play ball
on the green lawn

grown-ups for hours
eat and chat all at once
but they quiet down

when Grandpa tells how
one Sunday he first met
Grandma in Mexico

Grandpa's face
then shines a smile
bright like the Sun

DÍA FAMILIAR
por Francisco X. Alarcón

el día domingo
lo pasamos en casa
de nuestros abuelitos

junto con tíos y tías
muchos primitos
parientes y amigos

mientras los niños
nos ponemos a jugar
pelota en el jardín

los adultos por horas
comen y charlan todos
a la vez pero callan

cuando Abuelito cuenta
cómo un domingo conoció
a Abuelita en México

su cara entonces
reluce una sonrisa
radiante como el Sol

AT THE FARMER'S MARKET
by Buffy Silverman

A peach,
a pear,
a bag of beans,

Onions,
carrots,
lettuce greens.

Crispy,
crunchy,
juicy, sweet . . .

Pick your
favorite
veggie treat!

EN EL MERCADO DE AGRICULTORES
basado en "At the Farmers' Market"
por Buffy Silverman

Un durazno,
una pera,
una bolsa de frijoles.

Cebollas,
zanahorias,
lechugas frescas.

Crujientes,
crocantes,
jugosas, dulces . . .

Elige ya un vegetal,
¡y verás
que es un manjar!

SUMMER MELON
by Tricia Stohr-Hunt

Full of water
full of sweet
juicy, messy
treat to eat.

Dessert of summer
picnic jewel
ruby red and
oh so cool!

SANDÍA DE VERANO
basado en "Summer Melon"
por Tricia Stohr-Hunt

Llena de agua
llena de dulzura
jugosa y pringosa
delicia para comer.

Postre de verano
joya de *picnic*
rubí rojo y
¡oh, tan fresco!

IN RHYTHM
by Charles Waters

3-point shot in and *out*,
Rebound, outlet pass,
Fast break leads the way
Alley oop . . . Slam dunk!
Happy birthday NBA!

CON RITMO
basado en "In Rhythm"
por Charles Waters

Un tiro de tres puntos dentro y *fuera*,
Rebote, pase de salida,
Fast break—ataque rápido,
Alley-oop . . . ¡Clavada!
¡Feliz cumpleaños, NBA!

THANK YOU, DOLLAR
by Ann Whitford Paul

Happy Birthday, Dollar.
Today's your special day.
To celebrate, I'll spend you
on a yummy candy bar.
You are what I'll pay
so when I finish eating,
you will hear me say,
Thank you, thank you, Dollar.
You deserve this special day.

GRACIAS, DÓLAR
basado en "Thank You, Dollar"
por Ann Whitford Paul

Feliz cumpleaños, dólar.
Hoy es tu día especial.
Para celebrar, te gastaré
en una rica barra de dulce.
Tú eres lo que pagaré,
así que, cuando termine de comer,
oirás que te digo:
Gracias, gracias, dólar.
Te mereces este día especial.

BEWARE
by Kate Coombs

If you are an otter,
stay out of the water.

If you're a sardine,
try not to be seen.

If you are a ray,
please go away.

If you're a seahorse,
hide, of course.

From down underneath,
a flash of sharp teeth.

From down where it's dark,
the terrible shark.

A gray shape, a swish—
then goodbye, dear fish.

TEN CUIDADO
basado en "Beware"
por Kate Coombs

Si tú eres una nutria,
sal del agua con premura.

Si eres una sardina,
trata de estar escondida.

Si tú eres una raya,
vete ya porque algo pasa.

Si eres un caballito de mar,
ocúltate de inmediato.

Muy lejos, en el fondo,
destellan dientes filosos.

Desde la honda oscuridad,
el tiburón acecha sin piedad.

Sombra gris, huracán violento:
adiós, pez, de un mordisco hambriento.

LET'S CELEBRATE THE ELEPHANT!
by Irene Latham

What other animal

has a dump truck body
stuck on tree stump feet?

I like the way its skin
comes in shades of concrete.

See its hosepipe trunk
and sailboat ears?

Its tail is a windshield wiper
for its rear.

¡CELEBREMOS AL ELEFANTE!
basado en "Let's Celebrate the Elephant!"
por Irene Latham

¿Qué otro animal

tiene cuerpo de camión volcador
pegado sobre tocones?

Me gusta que su piel
viene en tonos de concreto.

¿Ves su trompa, como manguera,
y sus orejas, como veleros?

Su cola es un limpiaparabrisas
para su parte trasera.

THE VERY FIRST DAY OF SCHOOL
by Deborah Ruddell

Today is the day . . . a really big day . . .
The very first day of school!
    A Get-Yourself-Dressed Day
    A Looking-Your-Best Day
The very first day of school!

Today is the day . . . a really big day . . .
The very first day of school!
    A Brush-Your-Teeth-Quick Day
    A Camera-Click Day
The very first day of school!

EL PRIMER DÍA DE ESCUELA
basado en "The Very First Day of School"
por Deborah Ruddell

Hoy es el día, el gran día . . .
¡el primer día de escuela!
    El día de vestirse solo
    El día de verse espectacular
¡El primer día de escuela!

Hoy es el día, el gran día . . .
¡El primer día de escuela!
    El día de cepillarse rápido los dientes
    El día de sacarse fotos sonrientes
¡El primer día de escuela!

NO KIDDING!
by Michelle Schaub

Do riddles make you giggle?
Do knock knocks make you grin?
Do silly words and stories
give tickles to your skin?
If you tend to chuckle
when your funny bone is poked,
don't miss this day for kidding—
go share your favorite joke!

¡NO BROMEES!
basado en "No Kidding!"
por Michelle Schaub

¿Los acertijos te hacen reír?
¿Los chistes de toc toc te hacen sonreír?
¿Las palabras y los cuentos tontos
te hacen cosquillas en la piel?
Si te ríes entre dientes
cuando te golpeas el codo,
no te pierdas este día para bromear—
¡ve a compartir tu chiste preferido!

BOX FOR THE THRIFT SHOP
by April Halprin Wayland

My ma puts in her muffin tin,
I share the pants I can't fit in.
She adds our creaky baby gate.
I put in ragged Bear—oh, wait . . .

I know it's good to share our gear,
and things we haven't used all year,
but Bear says he's a toy to keep
if *someone* needs some help to sleep.

CAJA DE COSAS USADAS
basado en "Box for the Thrift Shop"
por April Halprin Wayland

Mamá pone el molde para panecillos,
yo, el pantalón que me queda chico.
Ella, nuestra puerta para bebés, que rechina.
Yo, el oso de peluche gastado—¡pero espera!

Aunque sé que es bueno compartir
y dar las cosas que no usamos más,
el oso dice que debe quedarse aquí
por si *alguien* necesita ayuda para dormir.

NATIONAL AVIATION DAY
by Tamera Will Wissinger

On National Aviation Day
we honor pilots, planes, and flight.
We celebrate two brothers:
Orville and Wilbur Wright.

They built a plane that they could steer—
it didn't travel very far.
Orville took off and landed quickly,
but still became a star.

That was in 1903—
now passengers can fly for miles.
Pilots navigate the planes, and
flight crews monitor the aisles.

Mechanics help keep planes in shape,
controllers guide and watch the skies.
It takes a team of many people
any time an airplane flies.

DÍA NACIONAL DE LA AVIACIÓN
basado en "National Aviation Day"
por Tamera Will Wissinger

En el Día Nacional de la Aviación,
honramos a los pilotos, aviones y vuelos,
y celebramos a dos hermanos,
Orville y Wilbur Wright,

por construir un avión que lograron manejar,
pero no llegó muy lejos.
Aunque Orville despegó y enseguida aterrizó,
pero aun se convirtió en una estrella.

Eso sucedió en 1903.
Ahora los pasajeros recorren millas en vuelo,
los pilotos conducen los aviones,
y la tripulación controla los pasillos.

Los mecánicos hacen el mantenimiento.
Los controladores aéreos guían y observan el cielo.
Se necesita que un gran equipo trabaje
cada vez que vuela una nave.

WAFFLES, WAFFLES, WAFFLES!
by Allan Wolf

From Birmingham to Baraboo
There is no better breakfast food.
Pass the maple syrup.
Give us waffles, waffles, waffles!

A waffle has a checkered face
To keep the butter in its place.
Pass the maple syrup.
Give us waffles, waffles, waffles!

Whenever we are in the mood
For pancakes with an attitude,
Pass the maple syrup.
Give us waffles, waffles, waffles!

¡WAFLES, WAFLES, WAFLES!
basado en "Waffles, Waffles, Waffles!"
por Allan Wolf

De Birmingham a Baraboo,
no hay mejor desayuno.
Pongan la miel de maple.
¡Dennos wafles, wafles, wafles!

Un wafle tiene cara cuadriculada
para que la mantequilla se quede en su lugar.
Pongan la miel de maple.
¡Dennos wafles, wafles, wafles!

Siempre que tengamos ganas
de panqueques con actitud,
pongan la miel de maple.
¡Dennos wafles, wafles, wafles!

MR. TICKLE-TOE
by J. Patrick Lewis

Mr. Tickle-Toe is a buttonhole cat,
And they don't get a whole lot smaller than that.

He isn't really skinny, no, he isn't really fat,
And he goes pitter-pat, pitter-pat, pat-pat.

He has a big room and he has a big bed,
But he has a little pillow for his wee little head.

And on his kitty plate is a wonderful fish,
So somebody guessed his birthday wish.

And in his kitty bowl is a Tickle-Toe dream—
Six blueberries swimming in buttermilk cream.

And he purrs at his owner as he hugs her shoe,
Which is Tickle-Toe talk—*I love you, too!*

EL SEÑOR COSQUILLITAS
basado en "Mr. Tickle-Toe" por J. Patrick Lewis

El señor Cosquillitas es un gato de ojal,
nada más pequeño se puede encontrar.

En verdad no es flaco; no es gordo, en verdad;
y sus pasos tamborilean, pin pan, pin pan, pan pan.

Tiene un cuarto grande y tiene una cama grande,
pero una almohada chiquita, para su diminuta cabecita.

En su plato de gato hay un magnífico pescado,
porque alguien adivinó su deseo de cumpleaños.

Y en su bol de gato hay un sueño de Cosquillitas:
crema de leche con seis arándanos nadando.

Y le ronronea a su dueño mientras le abraza el zapato,
que en idioma de gato significa—*¡Yo también te amo!*

BRAVE DOG!
by Stephanie Calmenson

There's Mr. Brown
And his guide dog, Skye.
They're crossing the street.
It's not time to say hi.

Oh, no—a car's turning—
Way too fast!
Skye stops Mr. Brown
Till the car goes past.

They're safely across now
So you can say hi
To your friend Mr. Brown
And his brave dog Skye.

¡PERRO VALIENTE!
basado en "Brave Dog!"
por Stephanie Calmenson

Ahí está el señor Brown
con su perro guía, Skye.
Mientras cruzan la calle,
no los debes saludar.

¡Oh, no, dobla un auto,
mira qué rápido!
Skye detiene a su amo
para que no le haga daño.

Ya cruzaron, están a salvo,
ahora puedes saludar
a tu amigo el señor Brown
y a su valiente perro, Skye.

FAR AWAY ON GRANDPARENTS DAY
by Julie Larios

I call my grandparents
Bebo and Beba—
that's short for *abuelo*
and short for *abuela*.
I like Bebo's photos,
I like Beba's smiles.
They send me *besitos*
across the long miles.

DESDE LEJOS, EN EL DÍA DE LOS ABUELOS
por Julie Larios

A mis abuelos los llamo
Bebo y Beba—
es más cortito que
Abuelo y Abuela.
Me gustan las fotos de mi bebo
y las sonrisas de mi beba.
Me mandan besitos
desde muy lejos.

WELCOME
by Linda Kulp Trout

Hello, neighbor!
What's your name?

Will you join
our kickball game?

Want half my cookie?
It's really good!

Welcome to the
neighborhood!

BIENVENIDO
basado en "Welcome"
por Linda Kulp Trout

¡Hola, vecino!
¿Cómo te llamas?

¿Jugarás con nosotros
un partido de *kickball*?

¿Quieres la mitad de mi galleta?
¡Está muy rica!

¡Bienvenido al
vecindario!

I CAN ASK AND I CAN LEARN
by Janet Wong

I am not Hispanic
but I can celebrate this month.
I asked my librarian
if she could teach us
a song in Spanish.
She sang *De Colores*
and talked to us about people
who joined together
and worked hard
to make farms better in California.

Even though I am not Hispanic
I felt so proud and happy
because I asked
and I learned.

PUEDO PREGUNTAR Y PUEDO APRENDER
basado en "I Can Ask and I Can Learn"
por Janet Wong

No soy hispano
pero puedo celebrar este mes.
Le pregunté a la bibliotecaria
si nos podía enseñar
una canción en español.
Cantó *De Colores*
y nos habló de gente
que se ha unido
y ha trabajado duro
para mejorar las granjas en California.

Aunque no soy hispano
me sentí tan orgulloso y feliz
porque pregunté
y aprendí.

ON THE MOON FESTIVAL
by Grace Lin

I am allowed to play
Outside tonight
Climb and slide and
SWING
Higher
Higher
I will knock on the moon
And the Moon Lady will say
Yes, tonight
The rabbit can come out to play.

Note: On the night of the Autumn-Moon Festival, people send the Moon Goddess or the Moon Lady a secret wish in hopes that she will grant it. The Moon Lady's companion is the Jade Rabbit.

EN EL FESTIVAL DE LA LUNA
basado en "On the Moon Festival"
por Grace Lin

Me dejan jugar
Afuera esta noche
Trepar y deslizarme y
COLUMPIARME
Más alto
Más alto
Tocaré a la puerta de la luna
Y la dama Luna dirá
Sí, esta noche
El conejo puede salir a jugar.

Nota: La noche del Festival de Medio Otoño, las personas le envían un deseo en secreto a la diosa Luna o dama Luna, con la esperanza de que ella se lo conceda. El compañero de la dama Luna es el Conejo Jade.

SAYS THE SEAGULL
by April Halprin Wayland

Who are these people on my pier?
I sail above them, then fly near.

They're singing, marching up the pier.
I think they did the same last year.

A father gives his girl some bread . . .
he smooths her hair then bows his head.

She watches waves, then tosses crumbs.
I dive, I catch, I swallow . . . yum!

A celebration on my pier—
I think I'll meet them every year!

Note: Tashlich (pronounced tash-leek or tash-lich) is celebrated during the Jewish New Year. In my hometown, we walk in a big, singing crowd to the pier, where we toss small pieces of bread into the sea for each mistake we made this past year. We say, "L'shanah Tovah!" which means "Good New Year!"

LA GAVIOTA DICE
basado en "Says the Seagull" por April Halprin Wayland

¿Quiénes son los que están en mi muelle?
Floto sobre ellas, después vuelo cerca.

Cantan y marchan por el muelle,
creo que hicieron lo mismo el año pasado.

Un padre da a su hija un poco de pan . . .
le alisa el cabello, luego inclina la cabeza.

Ella mira las olas, después arroja migas.
Yo me zambullo, las atrapo, las trago . . . ¡Qué ricas!

Una celebración en mi muelle—
¡creo que las encontraré todos los años!

Nota: Tashlich (pronunciado tash-leek o tash-lich) es celebrado durante el año nuevo judío. En mi ciudad natal caminamos en una gran multitud de canto hasta el muelle donde lanzamos pequeños pedazos de pan en el mar por cada error que hicimos el año pasado. Decimos "¡L'shanah Tovah!" que significa "¡Buen año nuevo!"

OUR BLENDED FAMILY
by Doraine Bennett

patchwork family
stitched together
by threads of love
a crazy quilt
of unexpected color

NUESTRA FAMILIA ENSAMBLADA
basado en "Our Blended Family"
por Doraine Bennett

familia de retazos
unidos con puntadas
de hilos de amor
una loca colcha
de inesperado color

A DREAM COME TRUE
by Georgia Heard

I covered my heart with my hand,
Sang "America the Beautiful," *From sea to shining sea* . . .
To celebrate my mom, my dad, my brother and me,
Becoming citizens of this great land.

I covered my heart with my hand,
Tears filled my eyes with pride and glory.
A dream come true, a brand new story,
Becoming citizens of this great land.

UN SUEÑO HECHO REALIDAD
basado en "A Dream Come True"
por Georgia Heard

Con la mano en el pecho,
Canté "America the Beautiful," *From sea to shining sea* . . .
Para celebrar que mamá, papá, mi hermano y yo
Nos hicimos ciudadanos de esta hermosa tierra.

Con la mano en el pecho
Y lágrimas de orgullo y gloria,
Un sueño se hizo realidad, una nueva historia,
Nos hicimos ciudadanos de esta hermosa tierra.

PIRATE TALK
by Robyn Campbell

First you need a pirate costume:
eye patch, hook, and big black hat.
Grab that skull-and-crossbones flag.
Don't forget your treasure map!
Say *aye aye* instead of *yes*.
Wave and shout *Ahoy* for *Hey!*
Say *avast* when you mean *Stop!*
What will be your pirate name?
Captain Longbeard? One-eyed Jack?
Don't forget to find a crew:
Parrots, monkeys, crocodiles—
teddy bears and puppies, too!

IDIOMA DE PIRATAS
basado en "Pirate Talk"
por Robyn Campbell

Primero necesitas un traje de pirata:
parche en el ojo, garfio y gran sombrero negro.
Sujeta esa bandera de una calavera.
¡No olvides tu mapa del tesoro secreto!
Di *a la orden, señor* en vez de *sí*.
Saluda y grita *¡Ah del barco!* en vez de *¡Hola!*
Di *¡Arrrr!* en vez de *¡Alto!*
¿Cuál será tu nombre de pirata?
¿Capitán Barba Larga? ¿El Juan-Tuerto?
No te olvides de encontrar una tripulación:
loros, monos, cocodrilos,
¡osos y perritos de peluche también!

BAND-AID CURE
by Bridget Magee

run
trip
tears drip

scrape
cut
eyes shut

Mom
comes
soft hums

cleans
knee
hugs me

love
pure
Band-Aid cure

REMEDIO: TIRITA ADHESIVA
basado en "Band-Aid Cure"
por Bridget Magee

corro
tropezón
las lágrimas brotan

raspón
corte
los ojos se cierran

viene
Mamá
suave tararea

limpia
la rodilla
me abraza

amor
puro
remedio: curita

Note: Band-Aid is a registered trademark of Johnson & Johnson.

LEAF DANCE
by David L. Harrison

Belly flopper
Into leaves,
They're in my hair
And up my sleeves.

Rustle crackle,
Crispy whirl,
Twisty jerky,
Crunchy swirl.

In my shirt
And down my pants,
Scritchy scratchy
Scrunchy dance,

Jumpy hoppy
Leap and sprawl.
Holler!
Scream!
Hooray for fall!

DANZA DE LAS HOJAS
basado en "Leaf Dance"
por David L. Harrison

Caigo de panza
Sobre las hojas,
Están en mi cabello,
Están sobre mis mangas.

Susurro crujiente,
Giro quebradizo,
Vuelta temblorosa,
Crocante remolino.

En la camisa,
En los pantalones,
Danza rechinante,
Crocante, chirriante.

Salto, reboto,
Me tiendo.
¡Grito!
¡Chillo!
¡Viva el otoño!

AS HIGH AS MOUNT EVEREST
by Margarita Engle

The ping swings of Nepal
are so extremely tall
that even grownups
look like tiny dolls
when they're way up
in the sky
flying!

Note: The tallest mountain in the world is Mount Everest, in
Nepal. During the October Dashain festival, both children and
adults enjoy swinging on enormous bamboo swings known as
pings.

TAN ALTO COMO LA MONTAÑA EVEREST
por Margarita Engle

¡En Nepal los columpios "ping"
son tan altísimos
que hasta los adultos
parecen muñequitas
mientras andan allá arriba
en el cielo
volando!

Nota: La montaña más alta del mundo es Everest, en Nepal.
Durante las fiestas Dashain en octubre, los niños y los adultos
gozan de columpios de bambú que son grandísimos, y que se
llaman "ping".

MY PIÑATA PARTY
by Margarita Engle

Stand back!
Watch out!
My turn to spin!
My turn to strike!
My turn to win!

When the candy falls
there will be plenty to share
but for now
BEWARE!

Note: Throughout Latin America, hollow papier-mâché statues are hung from tree branches so that blindfolded children can take turns trying to break them with broom handles or other big sticks to release colorfully wrapped pieces of candy hidden inside. The piñata is used at birthdays and other parties, always with adult supervision. Typically, a parent spins the blindfolded child around several times, then helps the child aim in the direction of the piñata. Once the candy falls, all the children scramble to get their share.

MI FIESTA DE LA PIÑATA
por Margarita Engle

¡Atras!
¡Cuidado!
¡Me toca a mí dar las vueltas!
¡Me toca a mí golpear!
¡Me toca a mí ganar!

Cuando se caen los dulces
habrán bastantes para compartir,
pero por ahora
¡CUIDADO!

Nota: Las piñatas se encuentran cuando celebran los cumpleaños y otras fiestas, donde se cuelga de la rama de un árbol. Los niños vendados tratan de quebrar la piñata con una escoba u otro palo grande, para que se caigan los dulces escondidos adentro.

DINOSAUR DINNERS
by Avis Harley

If dinosaurs were looking for a tasty treat,
how would we know what they liked to eat?

Fresh flesh? Or plants? What did they choose?
Scientists are always searching for clues.

Sharp, pointy teeth mean meat-eating beasts,
while thick, flat molars tell of plant-eating feasts.

The stomach of a skeleton is hard to find,
but it holds the last meal on which dino dined.

And amazing information lies in a scoop
of beautiful, fossilized dinosaur poop!

CENA DE DINOSAURIOS
basado en "Dinosaur Dinners" por Avis Harley

¿Qué comían los dinosaurios si querían darse un festín?
¿Cómo lo podríamos descubrir?

¿Carne fresca? ¿Vegetales? ¿Qué elegían?
Los científicos están siempre buscando pistas.

Los dientes filosos indican que comían carne;
los molares gruesos y planos, que comían vegetales.

El estómago de un esqueleto es difícil de encontrar,
pero podría contener la última cena del animal.

Se puede hallar asombrosa información
¡en restos hermosos y fosilizados de popó!

THE ROLLERBEARS
by Jack Prelutsky

In grassy fields, the Rollerbears
Are rolling up and down.
Their days are free, they have no cares,
They never wear a frown.
They roll in spring and summer,
And they roll throughout the fall,
And never give a single thought
To anything at all.

When winter comes, the Rollerbears
Roll straight into their dens,
To rest their weary wheels awhile,
And snooze till winter ends.
As soon as spring returns again,
And snows are off the ground,
The Rollerbears awaken
And begin to roll around.

LOS PATINETOSOS
basado en "The Rollerbears" por Jack Prelutsky

En los campos cubiertos de hierba,
Los Patinetosos ruedan de aquí para allá.
Sus días son libres, sin preocupaciones
Ni malos humores.
En la primavera
El verano y el otoño, ruedan
Sin detenerse
Un minuto a pensar.

Cuando llega el frío, los Patinetosos
Ruedan directo a su osera
Para que descansen un rato sus ruedas
Y hasta el fin del invierno duerman una siesta.
Al regresar la primavera,
Cuando la nieve desaparece de la tierra,
Los Patinetosos se despiertan
Y vuelven a rodar de aquí para allá.

MAKE A JOYFUL NOISE
by B.J. Lee

Pick on a banjo.
Bang on a drum.
What sound does it make?
Rum-tum-tum.

Shake some maracas.
Clack some sticks.
Grab your guitar
and play some licks.

Open your mouth
and sing a song,
or toot your kazoo
the whole day long.

SONIDOS ALEGRES
basado en "Make a Joyful Noise"
por B. J. Lee

Toca el banjo.
Percute el tambor.
¿Qué sonido tendrá?
Plan rataplán.

Sacude las maracas.
Repica los palillos.
Toma tu guitarra
y puntea las cuerdas.

Abre bien la boca,
entona una canción
o resopla el mirlitón
cada día a toda hora.

BEEP, BEEP, BEEP!
by Suzy Levinson

Make a fire safety plan!
First thing you should know . . .
smoke alarms say *beep, beep, beep*!
That means you should go!

Pick a nearby meeting place,
a mailbox or a tree.
Just as quick as *beep, beep, beep*,
join your family.

Why not practice more than one
method of escape?
Then if there's a *beep, beep, beep*,
you're in tip-top shape!

¡PIIP, PIIP, PIIP!
basado en "Beep, Beep, Beep!"
por Suzy Levinson

¡Los incendios hay que prevenir!
Primero debes saber . . .
el detector de humo suena *¡piip, piip, piip!*
¡Esto significa que debes correr!

Elige un lugar de reunión,
sea un árbol o un buzón,
y ve con tu familia hasta allí,
cuando oigas el *piip, piip, piip*.

Si practicas desde ahora
el método para huir,
¡estarás en mejor forma
cuando suene el *piip, piip, piip*!

WORLD EGG DAY
by Susan Blackaby

Today is Egg Day! Have you tried them
scrambled, deviled, poached, or fried?
Yummy eggs are on your plate,
but there are more! Let's celebrate
eggs in nests and streams and hives,
eggs on farms and eggs in cities;
egg-shaped eggs of every size,
ginormous down to itty-bitty;
ostrich eggs, like bowling balls,
or whale shark eggs (they're even bigger);
insect eggs that are so small
you need to use a magnifier;
and every egg that's in between
in every shade—white, brown, blue, green—
smooth or speckled, dry or wet,
E!G!G!S! Eggs! You bet!

DÍA MUNDIAL DEL HUEVO
basado en "World Egg Day" por Susan Blackaby

¡Hoy es el Día del Huevo! ¿Los probaste
revueltos, endiablados, escalfados o fritos?
Los deliciosos huevos están en tu plato,
¡pero aún hay más! Celebremos los huevos
en nidos y en corrientes y en colmenas,
los huevos en granjas y los huevos en ciudades;
los huevos con forma de huevo de cualquier tamaño,
desde gigantes hasta insignificantes,
huevos de avestruz, como bolos de boliche,
o de tiburón ballena (todavía más grandes)
hasta los huevos de insectos, que son tan pequeños
que necesitas una lupa para verlos,
y todos los huevos que hay entre ellos;
de todos los colores: blancos, azules, verdes, marrones,
lisos o manchados, secos o húmedos.
¡H U E V O S! ¡Huevos! ¡Que no te queden dudas!

THE DAY AFTER NATIONAL DESSERT DAY
by Charles Ghigna

I ate a bowl of jelly beans
For breakfast yesterday,
Then downed a dish of doughnut holes
To start the sweet buffet.

For lunch I ate a tray of treats,
Of cookies, tarts, and pie,
And then I baked a chocolate cake
With icing piled high.

For dinner I prepared a pot
Of sticky homemade stew,
With Jell-O, fudge, and jars of jam,
And other gobs of goo.

This morning I must take a break
And stay right here instead.
Dessert Day has finally passed—
And I am sick in bed!

EL DÍA SIGUIENTE AL DÍA NACIONAL DEL POSTRE
basado en "The Day After National Dessert Day" por Charles Ghigna

En el desayuno de ayer,
comí un tazón de habas de jalea,
un plato de centros de donuts después,
para empezar con el dulce buffet.

En el almuerzo, comí una bandeja
de galletas, tartas y manjares.
Luego horneé un pastel de chocolate
con el glaseado amontonado.

Para la cena preparé una olla
de guiso casero y gomoso,
con gelatina, caramelo, mermelada
y un montón de ingredientes pegajosos.

Ahora me tomaré un descanso,
me quedaré aquí por la mañana,
el Día del Postre ya ha pasado,
¡y yo me siento mal, estoy en cama!

BUBBLES
by Jacqueline Jules

Wiggle the soap!
Make some bubbles!
Wash away
germs and troubles.

Twenty seconds
is all it takes
to chase away
a stomachache.

BURBUJAS
basado en "Bubbles"
por Jacqueline Jules

¡A frotar el jabón!
¡Haz muchas burbujas!
Así los microbios
y penas repulsas.

Sólo veinte segundos
se necesitan
para alejar
dolor de pancita.

WHEN TO EAT PAN DULCE . . .
by René Saldaña, Jr.

On a cold Saturday morning
When Abuelita has brewed
A cup of hot chocolate
For me to warm my hands,
She places a plate on the table,
A tower of Mexican sweet breads:
Conchas, pan de polvo,
Churros and empanadas.
But my favorite
Is the cochinito,
A gingerbread piggy.
I pull it from the top of the tower,
Bring it to my nose,
Smell its oinky wonderfulness . . .
That's when I know
It's time to eat pan dulce.

CUÁNDO SE COME PAN DULCE . . .
basado en "When to Eat Pan Dulce . . ." por René Saldaña, h.

Un frío sábado por la mañana,
después de prepararme
una taza de chocolate caliente
para calentar mis manos,
mi abuelita pone en la mesa una bandeja
con una torre de delicias dulces mexicanas:
conchas, pan de polvo,
churros y empanadas.
Pero mi preferido
es el cochinito,
un cerdito de pan de jengibre.
Lo tomo de la cima de la torre,
me lo acerco a la nariz,
huelo su exquisito aroma . . .
Entonces sé que ha llegado
la hora de comer pan dulce.

DICTIONARY DOINGS
by Susan Marie Swanson

1.
Noah Webster collected words
before computers
and even before pens we buy in a store.
He wrote page after page
of words people say.
He trimmed a goose feather
and dipped that quill in a bottle of ink
to write words that we wonder with,
words that we think.

2.
The dictionary is a kitchen
where forks are kept in a drawer
with footballs, fruit, and flashlights.
The dictionary is a big box of tools
that belongs to everyone.
The dictionary is a place
where words stop to rest
on their way to meet you.

HECHOS DEL DICCIONARIO
basado en "Dictionary Doings" por Susan Marie Swanson

1.
Noah Webster recolectó palabras
antes de que hubiera computadoras
y hasta antes de los lápices que ahora se compran.
Llenó páginas y páginas
con palabras que decían las personas.
Recortó una pluma de ganso,
mojó la punta en un frasco de tinta
y con ella escribió las palabras que imaginamos,
las palabras que pensamos.

2.
El diccionario es una cocina
con un cajón donde se guardan tenedores
junto a trofeos, tomates y tijeras.
El diccionario es una gran caja de herramientas,
y todas las personas son sus dueñas.
El diccionario es un lugar
donde las palabras se detienen a descansar
cuando van camino a ti.

READY FOR SPAGHETTI
by Carrie Finison

When I'm ready for spaghetti
macaroni just won't do.
I say *No!* to rigatoni
and to fettuccine, too.

I don't want a bowl of bow-ties,
curlicues or tubes or rings,
or wagon wheels or seashells.
Give me pasta shaped like strings!

It's the perfect shape for slurping—
that's spaghetti etiquette.
I can never get enough!
Is my spaghetti ready yet?

PREPARADA PARA ESPAGUETIS
basado en "Ready for Spaghetti"
por Carrie Finison

Cuando estoy esperando espaguetis
los macarrones no me sirven.
Digo ¡no! a los regatones
y también a los fetuchines.

No quiero una taza de corbatines,
ni de coditos, tubos o anillos,
ni de rueditas o caracolas.
¡Denme pasta con forma de cordel!

Es la forma perfecta para sorber:
esa es la cualidad de los espaguetis.
¡Nunca son para mí suficientes!
¿Ya están listos mis espaguetis?

DEEPAVALI★ SOUNDS
by Uma Krishnaswami

Takku takku!
Visitors at the door
on Deepavali morning.

Chala chala!
My mother sprinkles water
on the ground, then draws the kolam,
rice-flour squares and circles,
dots and dabs and lotus flowers.

Gana gana gana!
The temple bells ring.
Oil lamps flicker on.

Karukku Murukku!
Special snacks,
crisp and crunchy.

Thattaar! Thattaar!
Firecrackers
burst into the night.

*also called Diwali for short

SONIDOS DE DEEPAVALI★
basado en "Deepavali* Sounds"
por Uma Krishnaswami

¡Takku takku!
Hay visitantes en la puerta
la mañana de *Deepavali.*

¡Chala chala!
Mi madre rocía el suelo
con agua, luego dibuja el *kolam*
con harina de arroz: cuadrados y círculos,
puntos y toques, y flores de loto.

¡Gana gana gana!
Suenan las campanas del templo.
Las lámparas de aceite titilan.

¡Karukku Murukku!
Comidas especiales,
crujientes y crocantes.

¡Thattaar! ¡Thattaar!
Los petardos
estallan a la noche.

*también abreviado como Diwali

TONIGHT
by Amy Ludwig VanDerwater

I am dressed up in my costume
from my head down to my feet.

I am ringing many doorbells.
I am saying *Trick or Treat!*

I am getting lots of candy.
I am thanking everyone.

I am friends with ghosts and witches.
Halloween is so much fun!

ESTA NOCHE
basado en "Tonight"
por Amy Ludwig VanDerwater

Me vestí con mi disfraz
de los pies a la cabeza.

Estoy tocando a muchas puertas
y diciendo *¡Dulce o truco!*

Me dan cantidad de dulces.
A todos les agradezco.

Soy amiga de fantasmas y de brujas.
¡El Día de Brujas es muy divertido!

THANK YOU! ¡GRACIAS!

BIRTHDAY
by Joan Bransfield Graham

Every year
on my birthday
hundreds
make a scene,
celebrate,
dress up,
stay out late,
give gifts,
but wait—
did I mention
my birthday's on
HALLOWEEN?

CUMPLEAÑOS
basado en "Birthday"
por Joan Bransfield Graham

Cada año
en mi cumpleaños,
cientos de personas
hacen decoraciones,
celebran,
se disfrazan,
andan por la calle
hasta altas horas,
reparten regalos.
¿Olvidé decirte
que mi cumpleaños
es el DÍA DE BRUJAS?

MAKING BREAD
by Debbie Reese

Outside
Thehtáy builds a fire in the pânteh.

Inside
Sá'yâa kneads the dough.

And me?
I help!

Outside, I throw sticks in the pânteh.
Inside, I shape loaves in baking tins.

Soon, cousins and aunties and me—
we carry twelve tins to the pânteh.

Thehtáy seals the door and we wait.
The smell makes it hard to wait, wait, wait!

When it is ready
Thehtáy opens the door.

Sá'yâa uses her wooden paddle
to slide the loaves out.

Hot bread.
Mmm, mmm, mmm.

Kų́'daa, Thehtáy!
Kų́'daa, Sá'yâa!

Note: For Pueblo peoples, making bread is a daylong, joyful family event sprinkled with Tewa words that mean Grandma (Sá'yâa), Grandpa (Thehtáy), oven (pânteh), and thank you (kú'daa).

Pronunciation guide:

Thehtáy = Te-Te, like in ten	Kų́'daa = Coot-dah
Sá'yâa = Sawt-yaw	Pânteh = Pond-Te

PREPARAMOS PAN
basado en "Making Bread" por Debbie Reese

Afuera
en la pânteh Thehtáy enciende el fuego.

Adentro
Sá'yâa prepara la masa.

¿Y yo?
¡Ayudo!

Afuera, en la pânteh, echo ramas.
Adentro, en los moldes, armo las barras.

A la pânteh llevamos enseguida
doce moldes, con mis primos y mis tías.

Thehtáy cierra la puerta, el pan se va a cocinar.
¡Con ese aroma es difícil esperar, y esperar, y esperar!

Cuando está listo
Thehtáy abre la puerta.

Sá'yâa usa la pala de madera
para sacar los panes fuera.

Pan caliente.
¡Mmm, mmm, mmm!

Kų́'daa, Thehtáy!
Kų́'daa, Sá'yâa!

Nota: Para los pueblos Pueblo, preparando pan es un actividad de familia durante todo el día y salpicado de palabras de Tewa, como Sá'yâa (Abuelita), Thehtáy (Abuelito), pânteh (estufa) y kú'daa (gracias).

Guía para la pronunciación:

Thehtáy = Teté	Kų́'daa = Cut-daa
Sá'yâa = Suat-ia	Pânteh = Pand-te

AT OUR HOUSE
by Virginia Euwer Wolff

Dad reads to me while he makes me lunch,
Mom reads to me in bed.
My little brother wants to hear
every word that we have read.

Grandpa's learning how to read,
Grandma hums along.
Books speak right up in our house,
and words turn into song.

EN CASA
basado en "At Our House"
por Virginia Euwer Wolff

Papi me lee mientras almuerzo,
Mami, cuando me acuesto.
Mi hermanito quiere oír
cada palabra que leemos.

Mi abuelito está aprendiendo a leer,
mi abuelita tararea alrededor.
Los libros hablan en casa,
y las palabras se hacen canción.

VOTING

by Diane Mayr

Step in a line.
Someone hands you a ballot.
Then you'll head into a booth.
Pull a curtain.
Think carefully.
Make a choice.

Vote for a man or woman
To do a job—
An important job.
To run your town,
Or your state,
Or your country.

Turn in your ballot.
Your vote will be counted,
A winner will be named.
You have done your duty,
Made your voice heard,
A citizen voting on Election Day.

VOTACIÓN

basado en "Voting" por Diane Mayr

Esperas en fila.
Te dan una boleta de una pila.
Vas despacio a la cabina.
Cierras muy bien la cortina.
Con cuidado determinas
por quién te inclinas.

Votas por un hombre o una mujer
para que cumpla
una tarea importante
en el gobierno de tu pueblo,
tu estado
o tu país.

Entregas la boleta.
Tu voto contarán.
Dirán quién ganó en esa ocasión.
Cumpliste tu obligación,
y se escuchó tu voz
el Día de la Elección.

COME AND PLAY
by Anastasia Suen

It's International Games Day!
Which game will you play?

circle games
board games
parachute games
floor games

Come and play a game
with the friends you see.
We're playing games together
at our library.

puppet games
rhyming games
dress-up games
video games

It's International Games Day!
Come and play!

VEN A JUGAR
basado en "Come and Play"
 por Anastasia Suen

¡Es el Día Internacional del Juego!
¿A qué jugarás?

Juegos en círculo,
juegos de mesa,
juegos con paracaídas,
juegos en el piso.

Ven a jugar
con los amigos que ves.
Jugamos todos juntos
en nuestra biblioteca.

Juegos con títeres,
juegos con rima,
juegos con disfraces,
juegos de video.

¡Es el Día Internacional del Juego!
¡Ven a jugar!

ON THE DAY OF THE DEAD
by René Saldaña, Jr.

At the foot of his grave,
We spread out a blanket—
Rough but my Abuelo's favorite,
Still bright and colorful.
Abuela places
Their wedding photo
At the head,
Just under his name
Carved into granite.
'Amá lays down flowers and
His favorite coffee mug.
Next, Tío Ernesto sets
A plate and a napkin.
Followed by a string
Of us nietos and nietas,
Who bring the food and drinks:
Pan de muerto,
Mexican hot chocolate,
And for the grown-ups
Café de olla.
We serve him first—
A piece of bread
And a steaming cup
Of coffee, a cinnamon stick
For stirring—
Then we whisper our messages,
Like we used to on his lap
Just last year,
And he'd whisper back
His sweet-everythings.
We sit and eat and think.

How we all miss him.

EN EL DÍA DE LOS MUERTOS
basado en "On the Day of the Dead"
por René Saldaña, h.

Al pie de la tumba de mi abuelo,
extendemos una cobija,
tosca, pero su preferida,
todavía brillante y colorida.
En la cabecera,
justo debajo de su nombre
grabado en el granito,
la abuela acomoda
la foto de su boda.
'Amá apoya las flores
y su taza de café predilecta.
Luego, tío Ernesto,
un plato y una servilleta;
y el torrente de nosotros,
nietos y nietas, damos
la comida y la bebida:
pan de muerto,
chocolate caliente mexicano
y para los mayores
café de olla.
Le servimos primero a él:
un trozo de pan,
una humeante taza de café,
una rama de canela
para revolver.
Le susurramos mensajes,
como hacíamos en su regazo
hace apenas un año,
y él retribuía
con dulces melodías.
Nos sentamos y comemos y pensamos.

Cuánto lo extrañamos.

THE EARL'S "INVENTION"
by Patricia Toht

I'm the Earl,
the *hungry* Earl.
I want something to eat!

I'm occupied
with playing cards—
no time to carve my meat.

Spread thick mustard,
stack some cheese,
and wrap it all in bread.

Forget the plate,
the fork and knife—
I'll use my hands instead.

Would you like
some food, my friends,
that won't disrupt our game?

Just order up
the same as me—
"Sandwich" is my name!

EL "INVENTO" DEL CONDE
basado en "The Earl's 'Invention'"
por Patricia Toht

Yo soy el conde,
el conde hambriento.
¡Quiero algo para comer!

Estoy ocupado
jugando a las cartas,
no tengo tiempo de cortar carne.

Esparza mostaza abundante,
póngale queso
y envuelva todo con pan.

Olvídese del plato
el tenedor y el cuchillo:
usaré las manos en su lugar.

Mis amigos,
¿quisieran comer algo
que no interrumpa nuestro juego?

Solo pidan
lo mismo que yo:
¡"Sándwich" es mi nombre!

DEAR VETERAN
by Linda Kulp Trout

You fought
for our freedom.
You kept our country safe.
Today we proudly honor you,
Hero.

QUERIDO VETERANO
basado en "Dear Veteran"
por Linda Kulp Trout

Luchaste
por nuestra libertad.
Nuestro país mantuviste a salvo.
Hoy con orgullo te honramos,
Héroe.

A BICYCLE BUILT FOR TEN
by J. Patrick Lewis

On a bicycle built for ten—
Be it boys and girls, women or men—
    You must pedal and pedal
    And pedal and pedal,
And then you must pedal again.

But here is the odd thing: At last,
No matter the records you've passed,
    Though you pedal and pedal
    And pedal and pedal,
You *cannot* go ten times as fast.

UNA BICICLETA PARA DIEZ PERSONAS
basado en "A Bicycle Built for Ten"
por J. Patrick Lewis

En una bicicleta para diez,
sean niños o niñas, mujeres u hombres,
    debes pedalear y pedalear
    y pedalear y pedalear
y luego pedalear de nuevo.

Pero esto es lo raro: al final,
sin importar los récords que hayas superado,
    a pesar de haber pedaleado y pedaleado
    y pedaleado y pedaleado,
no puedes ir diez veces más rápido.

RETIRED TIRES
by Neal Levin

Retired tires make good swings
And other neat recycled things
That lots of people often use:
Tables, sandals, tennis shoes,
Floormats, doormats, shingles, boots,
Trash bins, gravel substitutes,
Artificial reefs and rocks,
Bumpers tied to swimming docks,
Baskets, jewelry, purses, wallets,
Works of art and whatchamacallits.
Sometimes something new requires
Saving old retired tires.

NEUMÁTICOS VIEJOS
basado en "Retired Tires"
por Neal Levin

Los neumáticos viejos hacen buenos columpios
y sirven para otras cosas recicladas
que muchas personas suelen usar:
mesas, sandalias, tenis,
tapetes, felpudos, tejas, botas,
botes de basura, sustitutos de grava,
arrecifes y piedras artificiales,
parachoques amarrados a muelles de natación,
cestos, joyas, carteras, billeteras,
obras de arte y lo que sea.
A veces, para algo nuevo se necesita
rescatar los neumáticos viejos.

BUTTONS
by Penny Parker Klostermann

Buttons, buttons, shiny buttons—
buttons in a jar.
Lost-then-found ones,
square ones, round ones,
buttons shaped like stars.

Buttons, buttons, shiny buttons—
buttons on my clothes.
Coat ones, skirt ones,
on-my-shirt ones,
buttons sewn in rows.

Buttons, buttons, shiny buttons—
buttons cuddled tight.
Tucked-in snug ones,
teddy-hug ones.
Buttons wink goodnight.

BOTONES
basado en "Buttons" por Penny Parker Klostermann

Botones, botones, botones brillantes—
botones en un frasco.
Perdidos y luego encontrados,
cuadrados, redondos,
botones con forma de estrella.

Botones, botones, botones brillantes—
botones en mi ropa.
Los de abrigos, los de faldas,
los de mis camisas,
botones cosidos en fila.

Botones, botones, botones brillantes—
botones bien ajustados.
Los que abrigan,
los que son como abrazo de osito.
Los botones nos dan las buenas noches.

OUR FAMILY
by Kate Coombs

They look at my dad
and they look at my mom

and they're kind of confused,
like what's going on?

My mom's skin is pale.
Her eyes are blue.

But my skin is brown.
I'm from Peru.

My dad has freckles
and bright red hair.

My sister's from China,
my brother—Delaware.

Oh, you're adopted!
they finally say.

Yep! We're adopted.
We like it that way.

Is it strange? Is it special?
they whisper to me.

Nope. It's just us.
Our family.

NUESTRA FAMILIA
basado en "Our Family"
por Kate Coombs

Cuando miran a papá,
cuando miran a mamá,

parecen algo confundidos,
¿qué es lo que ha sucedido?

La piel de mamá es clara,
el color de sus ojos, azul.

Pero mi piel es oscura,
soy del Perú.

Mi papá tiene pecas
y cabello pelirrojo.

Mi hermana es de la China;
mi hermano, de Delaware.

¡Son adoptados, ah!
dicen al final.

¡Sip!, somos adoptados
y nos gusta ser así.

¿Es extraño? ¿Es especial?
me susurran a mí.

Nop. Solo somos nosotros.
Nuestra familia.

Note: Poet Kate Coombs is one of seven adopted children in a multiethnic family.
Nota: La poetisa Kate Coombs es uno de los siete hijos adoptados de una familia multiétnica.

A THANKSGIVING CHEER
by Brod Bagert

Sweet potato pie!
Sweet potato pie!
Momma gonna bake some sweet potato pie!

Cranberry sauce!
Cranberry sauce!
Poppa gonna make some cranberry sauce!

Turkey in the oven!
Turkey in the oven!
Granny got a big fat turkey in the oven.

Thanks is the word!
Thanks is the word!
THANKS I WAS NOT BORN A BIRD!

Cause if I were a bird, you see,
those humans would be roasting me.

Gobble gobble turkey Mama!
Gobble turkey Papa, too!

Gobble gobble turkey ME!
Gobble turkey YOU!

¡VIVA EL DÍA DE ACCIÓN DE GRACIAS!
basado en "A Thanksgiving Cheer"
por Brod Bagert

¡Pie de camote!
¡Pie de camote!
¡Mamá horneará pie de camote!

¡Salsa de arándanos!
¡Salsa de arándanos!
¡Papá cocinará salsa de arándanos!

¡Un pavo en el horno!
¡Un pavo en el horno!
¡La abuela puso un pavo enorme en la estufa!

¡La palabra es *gracias*!
¡La palabra es *gracias*!
¡PORQUE NO SOY AVE, DOY LAS GRACIAS!

Porque si yo fuera ave,
los seres humanos me asarían.

¡Glu glu mamá pavo!
¡Glu glu también papá pavo!

¡Glu glu pavo YO!
¡Glu glu pavo TÚ!

WINTER COUNTING
by Joseph Bruchac

How many winters
do you have?
That's how we ask
someone their age.

The snow that fell,
then melted away,
reminds us that
we still are here.

It's easy to count
your age by years.
We think winter counting
is a better way.

It makes us grateful
for the spring
when every bird
and every flower
welcomes us to
a whole new time.

Then sunshine is
in every heart
and we smile
as we ask each other
how many winters
do you have now?

CONTAR LOS INVIERNOS
basado en "Winter Counting"
por Joseph Bruchac

¿Cuántos inviernos
tienes?
Así le preguntamos
a alguien su edad.

La nieve caída,
que luego se derrite,
nos hace recordar
que estamos aquí todavía.

Es fácil contar tu edad
por los años,
pero pensamos que por inviernos
es mucho mejor.

Nos hace agradecer
por la primavera,
cuando todas las aves
y todas las flores
nos dan la bienvenida
a una etapa nueva.

Entonces la luz del sol
nos alumbra el corazón,
y con una sonrisa
nos preguntamos:
¿cuántos inviernos
tienes ahora?

CHANUKAH'S HERE!
by Lesléa Newman

Candles stand tall
Prayers said by all

Potatoes are pared
Latkes are shared

Sweet chocolate gelt
(Don't let it melt!)

New book and toy
For each girl and boy

Donuts are fried
New games are tried

Clay dreidel spins
Everyone wins!

¡LLEGÓ JANUKÁ!
basado en "Chanukah's Here!"
por Lesléa Newman

Las velas están en alto
Todos dicen oraciones

Se pelan las papas
Se comparten los buñuelos

Monedas de chocolate dulce
(¡No las dejes derretir!)

Un libro y un juguete nuevos
Para cada niño y niña

Se fríen las rosquillas
Se prueban otros juegos

Gira la perinola de arcilla
¡Todos ganan!

FRIENDS
by Renée M. LaTulippe

Annie
has a chair on wheels.
She's fast
and she can spin!
We race each other
after school.
Sometimes she lets me win.

Robert
doesn't talk like me,
but draws
a whole lot better.
He points out pictures
in our books,
and I point out each letter.

Lucy
moves her hands to speak,
her fingers
forming shapes.
We are silent
superheroes
in our masks and capes.

My friends and I
are different,
but not in every way.
All of us love having fun—
we read
and draw
and play!

AMIGOS
basado en "Friends"
por Renée M. LaTulippe

Annie
tiene una silla de ruedas.
¡Anda rápido
y da vueltas!
Corremos carreras
después de la escuela,
y, a veces, me deja ganar.

Robert
no habla como yo,
pero dibuja
muchísimo mejor.
Señala
los dibujos del libro,
y yo señalo cada letra.

Lucy
solo mueve las manos cuando habla,
forma figuras
con los dedos.
Somos superhéroes
silenciosos,
con máscara y capa.

Mis amigos y yo
somos diferentes,
aunque no completamente.
¡Todos queremos diversión—
leer
y dibujar
y jugar!

COOKIES!
by Cynthia Cotten

animal crackers,
oatmeal, fig,
peanut butter,
small or big

sugar, molasses,
thin or thick—
cookies always
do the trick

¡GALLETAS!
basado en "Cookies!"
por Cynthia Cotten

galletas de animalitos,
de avena, higos,
mantequilla de maní,
pequeñas o grandes

azúcar, melaza,
finas o gruesas—
las galletas siempre
satisfacen

TIGER
by Bruce Balan

A tiger is a brilliant beast
to stare at and admire
The colors of his fur are fierce
like thunderclouds and fire.

It's wonderful to watch him sleep
so peaceful and serene
But I'm not sure I'd feel this way
with no fence in between.

EL TIGRE
basado en "Tiger"
por Bruce Balan

El tigre es una bestia brillante
para mirar y admirar.
El color de su pelaje es feroz
como los nubarrones y el fuego.

Es maravilloso verlo dormir
tan pacífico y sereno,
pero no sé si me sentiría así
sin una reja de por medio.

LOOKING FOR A BOOK: A DIALOGUE WITH A LIBRARIAN
by Elizabeth Steinglass

Do you have any books
about chickens and chicks?

*Let's follow the numbers to
six thirty-six.*

I like reading stories
where wolves lie in wait.

*Traditional tales are marked
three ninety-eight.*

Can you tell me the name
of this rock in my shoe?

*For mineral guides, head to
five fifty-two.*

Why did the Pilgrims
sail over the sea?

*We'll spot what you need at
nine seventy-three.*

How do you know
where to find every book?

*Dewey numbered them all,
so we'd know where to look.*

BUSCANDO UN LIBRO: DIÁLOGO CON UNA BIBLIOTECARIA
basado en "Looking for a Book: A Dialogue with a Librarian" por Elizabeth Steinglass

¿Tiene libros
sobre pollos y polluelos para ver?

*Seguiremos los números hasta
el seiscientos treinta y seis.*

Me gusta leer historias
donde acechan lobos.

*Los cuentos tradicionales se marcan
con el trescientos noventa y ocho.*

¿Puede decirme el nombre
de la piedra que en mi zapato se metió?

*Para guías de minerales, ve
al quinientos cincuenta y dos.*

Los peregrinos
cruzaron el mar, ¿por qué?

*Encontraremos lo que necesitas
en el novecientos setenta y tres.*

¿Cómo sabe en qué lugar
hay que buscar cada libro?

*Dewey los numeró,
para que sepamos dónde están.*

CHEERING FOR COCOA
by Ken Slesarik

It's cocoa, it's cocoa, come on kids, let's go!
December 13th, it's the cocoa bean show!
It's cocoa, it's cocoa, we love you, hello,
on almonds, in pudding, and sweet cookie dough.
It's cocoa, it's cocoa, so sip, drink, or eat.
Hot cocoa in winter—my favorite treat!
It's cocoa, it's cocoa, I'm glad we could meet
and share yummy cocoa. It just can't be beat!

HURRA POR EL CACAO
basado en "Cheering for Cocoa"
por Ken Slesarik

¡Cacao, cacao, vengan, chicos, vamos!
¡Es 13 de diciembre, es el *show* del cacao!
Cacao, cacao, hola, te amamos
con almendras, en pudines y galletas.
Cacao, cacao, lo puedes sorber, beber o comer.
Cacao caliente en invierno: ¡mi bebida preferida!
Cacao, cacao, que lindo es que nos pudimos reunir
y lo podamos compartir. ¡No hay nada igual!

MY BLUE FLASHLIGHT
by Eileen Spinelli

I love my blue flashlight
when there is a wild storm
and the power goes out
and Mama says: *Where is your
blue flashlight?*
And suddenly the storm becomes
less scary all around.

MI LINTERNA AZUL
basado en "My Blue Flashlight"
por Eileen Spinelli

Me encanta mi linterna azul
cuando arrecia el temporal
y se corta la electricidad.
Entonces mamá pregunta:
Tu linterna azul, ¿dónde está?
Y, de pronto, la tormenta
ya no asusta más.

DECEMBER SOLSTICE
by Caroline Starr Rose

(Northern Hemisphere)

Welcome, winter,
longest night,
frozen mornings,
day's short light.

night's short song.
golden evenings,
sun runs long,
Hello, summer,

(Southern Hemisphere)

SOLSTICIO DE DICIEMBRE
basado en "December Solstice"
por Caroline Starr Rose

(Hemisferio norte)

Bienvenido, invierno,
la noche más larga,
mañanas heladas,
días más cortos.

la noche: corta canción.
tardes doradas,
horas y horas de sol,
Hola, verano,

(Hemisferio sur)

Note: When it comes to the seasons, our planet is an upside down, opposite sort of place.

Winter begins in the northern part of the world on the day called Winter Solstice (December 21, 22, or 23, depending on the year). Just as we begin winter in the United States, people who live in the southern hemisphere are starting summer.

Nota: En relación con las estaciones, en nuestro planeta hay lugares que están al revés, que son opuestos.

En la parte norte del mundo, el invierno empieza el día del solsticio de invierno (21, 22, o 23 de diciembre, según el año). Justo cuando en los Estados Unidos empezamos el invierno, quienes viven en el hemisferio sur empiezan el verano.

CHRISTMAS TREE
by Joseph Bruchac

The smell of Christmas is a tree,
a real tree brought inside.
It stands there in our living room,
its green branches spread wide.

Popcorn and candy both smell fine,
but not as good as that.
Covered with colored balls and lights,
it wears a star for a hat.

That tree makes me think of the woods
and walking in the snow.
I'm glad it's come to stay with us
for just a week or so.

EL ÁRBOL DE NAVIDAD
basado en "Christmas Tree"
por Joseph Bruchac

Navidad: aroma del árbol real
que traemos a casa
y ponemos en la sala,
con sus amplias y verdes ramas.

Las palomitas de maíz y los dulces huelen bien,
pero nunca como el árbol,
lleno de luces y adornos de colores,
con su estrella por sombrero.

Me recuerda a los bosques,
las caminatas en la nieve,
y estoy feliz de que al menos
una semana se quede.

BOXING DAY
by Monica Gunning

Want a Jamaican fun day?
Come the day after Christmas.
It's Boxing Day.
Need boxing gloves?
No way!
We play and eat
Christmas leftovers.
Curry goat and rice,
Corn pone with spice,
Coconut juice, so nice.
Frolic on the beach.
Cool off with shaved ice.
Whoop it up for Boxing Day!

Note: Boxing day started in England. It
was the day they boxed up Christmas day
leftovers for the poor.

DÍA DE LAS CAJAS
basado en "Boxing Day"
por Monica Gunning

¿Quieres un día jamaiquino divertido?
Ven al día siguiente de Navidad.
Es el *Boxing Day*.
¿Necesitas guantes de boxeo?
¡No!, porque es el Día de las Cajas,
cuando jugamos y comemos
las sobras de Navidad:
guiso de cabra con curry y arroz,
pan de maíz con especias,
agua de coco, tan rica.
En la playa hay diversión.
Los raspados de hielo refrescan.
Por el Día de las Cajas, ¡viva, viva!

Nota: El Día de las Cajas se originó en Inglaterra.
Era el día en que se les repartían cajas con lo que
había sobrado de Navidad a los pobres.

SEVEN CANDLES (MISHUMAA SABA)

by Carol-Ann Hoyte

Seven candles will shine bright
in the kinara tomorrow night
on the last and seventh night
of a festival called Kwanzaa.

*What color is the candle
standing in the center?*
This center candle is black
for the color of my people.

*What color are the candles
standing to the left?*
These left candles are red
for the struggle of my people.

*What color are the candles
standing to the right?*
These right candles are green
for the future of my people.

Seven candles will shine bright
in the kinara tomorrow night
on the last and seventh night
of a festival called Kwanzaa.

Note: Kwanzaa takes place from December 26 to January 1, when people all over the world celebrate African American and Pan-African history, culture, families, and community. Seven principles (ideas on how to live a good life) are honored during the seven days of Kwanzaa.

LAS SIETE VELAS (MISHUMAA SABA)

basado en "Seven Candles"
por Carol-Ann Hoyte

Las siete velas alumbrarán radiantes
en la kinara desde la noche de mañana
hasta la séptima y última noche
de un festival llamado Kwanzaa.

*¿De qué color es la vela
que está en el centro?*
Esta vela central es negra
por el color de mi pueblo.

*¿De qué color son las velas
de la izquierda?*
Estas velas de la izquierda son rojas
por la lucha de mi pueblo.

*¿De qué color son las velas
de la derecha?*
Estas velas de la derecha son verdes
por el futuro de mi pueblo.

Las siete velas alumbrarán radiantes
en la kinara desde la noche de mañana
hasta la séptima y última noche
de un festival llamado Kwanzaa.

Nota: Kwanzaa se festeja desde el 26 de diciembre hasta el 1 de enero, cuando personas de todo el mundo celebran la historia, la cultura, las familias y la comunidad afroamericana y panafricana. Durante los siete días de Kwanzaa se honran siete principios (normas para vivir una vida buena).

HAPPY NOON YEAR!
by Anastasia Suen

The old year is ending.
The time is near.
A new year is coming.
Let's welcome it here.

We'll play some games,
And wear party hats,
Sing and dance,
And eat party snacks.

Look at the clock,
It's almost noon.
Are you ready?
It's coming soon.

Let's count it down . . .
10
9
8
7
6
5
4
3
2
1!
Happy Noon Year!

¡FELIZ AÑO NUEVO AL MEDIODÍA!
basado en "Happy Noon Year!"
por Anastasia Suen

El año viejo llega a su fin.
La hora está cerca.
Un nuevo año está por venir.
Abrámosle la puerta.

Haremos algunos juegos,
con sombreros de fiesta,
cantaremos, bailaremos,
la comida está en la mesa.

Miren el reloj,
ya es casi mediodía.
¿Están preparados?
Llegará enseguida.

Vamos a contar . . .
¡10
9
8
7
6
5
4
3
2
1!
¡Feliz Año Nuevo al mediodía!

NOBODY'S BIRTHDAY!
by Marilyn Singer

It's nobody's birthday, but why should we wait?
There are thousands of things we can all celebrate.
Let's party for starfish and mushrooms and eagles.
Let's hoopla for hailstones and acorns and beagles.
Let's root for the grass and the whole Milky Way.
Let's cheer for the world each astonishing day.

¡EL CUMPLEAÑOS DE NADIE!
basado en "Nobody's Birthday!"
por Marilyn Singer

Es el cumpleaños de nadie, ¿pero por qué deberíamos esperar?
Hay miles de cosas para celebrar.
Festejemos por las estrellas de mar y los hongos y las águilas.
Que suenen bombos y platillos por el granizo y las bellotas y los sabuesos.
Gritemos hurra por el césped y por toda la Vía Láctea.
Animemos a el mundo cada extraordinario día.

100 Pieces	21
As High as Mount Everest	125
At Our House	141
At the Farmer's Market	102
At the Seder	45
Band-Aid Cure	123
Baseball's Opening Day	47
Beep, Beep, Beep!	130
Beware	106
Bicycle Built for Ten, A	147
Bicycle Dreams	64
Bilingual	31
Bilingual Daisy	29
Birthday	139
Birthday Tanka	22
Black History Month	24
Boats	95
Books	51
Box for the Thrift Shop	110
Boxing Day	162
Brave Dog!	114
Break an Egg	46
Break-Fast	88
Bubbles	133
Buttons	149
Camping	76
Car, Bus, Train, or Bike	83
Carnival Tuesday	27
Chanukah's Here!	153
Cheering for Cocoa	158
Children's Day, Book Day	60
Christmas Tree	161
Come and Play	143
Compliment Chain	20
Cookies!	155
Dancer, The	59
Day After National Dessert Day, The	132
Day to Honor Fathers, A	82
Daylight Saving Time	40
Dear Veteran	146
December Solstice	160
Deepavali Sounds	137
Dictionary Doings	135
Dinosaur Dinners	127
Dream Come True, A	121
Dream without Hunger, A	73
Earl's Invention, The	145
Earth, You Are	57
Fables	41
Family Day	101
Far Away on Grandparents Day	115
First Laugh, Navajo Baby	48
Friends	154
Happy Adoption Day	35
Happy Birthday, Dr. Seuss	38
Happy Noon Year!	164
Happy Pride!	86
Hats Off to Hat Day	16
How to Love Your Little Corner of the World	28
How to Make a Friend	99
I Am Not a Plucot	62
I Can Ask and I Can Learn	117
I Can Help!	13
I Scream!	98
I'm Bigger	53
In Rhythm	104
Independence Day	91
Jackson	78
Juneteenth	84
Just Weight!	52
Laughing	68
Leaf Dance	124
Let the Games Begin	92
Let's Celebrate the Elephant	107
Let's Go	65
Long Time Ago, A	36
Look for the Helpers	69
Looking for a Book: A Dialogue with a Librarian	157
Make a Joyful Noise	129
Making Bread	140

Marching Band of Vitamins, A   77
Martin's Birthday   18
Moon Walk—July 21, 1969   96
Mom's Perfume   71
Mr. Groundhog   26
Mr. Tickle-Toe   113
My 100th Day Collection   17
My Blue Flashlight   159
My Graduation   75
My Piñata Party   126
My Place to Fly   54
National Aviation Day   111
National Hammock Day   97
New Year Cheer   23
New Year Is Here   12
No Kidding!   109
Nobody's Birthday!   165
Obon   94
Oh Summer Books   79
On Halfway Day   90
On National Engineers Week   33
On the Day of the Dead   144
On the Moon Festival   118
Our Blended Family   120
Our Family   150
Paper Bag Is Never Empty, A   93
Pet Week Show-and-Tell   66
Picky Eater   39
Picnic Chant   89
Pirate Talk   122
Pizza Week Menu   15
Pocket Change   56
Pocket Poems™ Card   58
Poet Celebrates National   10
  Soup Month., The
Popcorn Party   19
Presidents' Day   30
Reading Braille   11
Ready for Spaghetti   136
Recipe for a Twin Birthday   74
Red, White, and Blue   81
Retired Tires   148

Rollerbears, The   128
Says the Seagull   119
Selfie   63
Seven Candles   163
Sincerely   37
Some Reasons to Write a Poem   49
Spring   43
St. Patrick's Day   42
STOP! Let's Read!   55
Summer in Alaska   85
Summer Melon   103
Super Bowl Sunday   25
Teacher Knows, A   67
Thank You, Dollar   105
Thanksgiving Cheer, A   151
Things Not to Do   72
Thinking about World Thinking Day   32
Three Kings Day   14
Tiger   156
Today's the Day!   100
Tonight   138
Treasure Hunt   70
Tree Day Celebration   50
Very First Day of School!, The   108
Voting   142
Waffles, Waffles, Waffles!   112
Welcome   116
What Will You Choose, Baby?   61
When to Eat Pan Dulce   134
Winter Counting   152
Wishes Around the World   87
World Egg Day   131
World Water Day   44
Yo-Yo   80
You Can Call Me   34

100 piezas	21
Afectuosamente	37
Algunas razones para escribir un poema	49
¡ALTO! A leer	55
Amigos	154
árbol de Navidad, El	161
Auto, autobús, tren o bicicleta	83
Autofoto	63
Bailarín, El	59
banda de vitaminas, Una	77
Bebé, ¿qué elegirás?	61
Bienvenido	116
Bilingüe	31
bolsa de papel nunca está vacía, Una	93
Botes	95
Botones	149
Burbujas	133
Busca a los ayudantes	69
Buscando un libro: Diálogo con una bibliotecaria	157
Búsqueda del tesoro	70
Cadena de cumplidos	20
Caja de cosas usadas	110
Caminata lunar: 21 de julio de 1969	96
Campamento	76
Canción del picnic	139
celebración del Día del árbol, La	50
¡Celebramos al Elefante!	107
Cena de dinosaurios	127
Cómo amar tu pequeño rincón del mundo	28
Cómo hacerse de un amigo	99
Con ritmo	104
Contar los inviernos	152
Cosas que no se hacen	72
Cuándo se come pan dulce . . .	134
Cumpleaños	139
cumpleaños de Martin, El	18
cumpleaños de nadie!, ¡El	165
Danza de las hojas	124
"Desayuno" por la noche	88
Desde lejos, en el Día de los Abuelos	115
Deseos por todo el mundo	87
Día de inauguración de la temporada de béisbol	47
Día de la Independencia	91
Día de las Cajas	162
día de los niños, El día de los libros, El	60
Día de los Presidentes	30
Día de San Patricio	42
Día familiar	101
Día Mundial del Agua	44
Día Mundial del Huevo	131
Día Nacional de la Aviación	111
Día Nacional de la Hamaca	97
día para honrar a los padres, Un	82
día siguiente al Día Nacional del Postre, El	132
Domingo de Supertazón	25
En casa	141
En el Día de los Muertos	144
En el festival de la luna	118
En el mercado de agricultores	102
En el Séder	45
En la mitad del día	90
En la Semana Nacional de los Ingenieros	33
Esta noche	138
Exigente para comer	82
Fábulas	41
Feliz Año Nuevo al MEDIODÍA!	164
Feliz cumpleaños, Dr. Seuss	38
Feliz día de la adopción	35
¡Feliz Día del Orgullo!	86
Fiesta de palomitas de maíz	19
¡Galletas!	155
gaviota dice, La	119
Gracias, dólar	105
¡Grito!	98
Hace mucho tiempo	36
Hechos del diccionario	135
Horario de verano	40
¡Hoy es el día!	100

Hurra por el cacao	158
Idioma de piratas	122
"Invento" del Conde, El	145
Jackson	78
Juneteenth	84
Leer en braille	11
Libros de verano	79
libros, Los	51
Llegó el Año Nuevo	12
¡Llegó Januká!	153
maestro sabe, Un	67
Margarita bilingüe	29
Martes de Carnaval	27
Menú semanal de pizza	15
Mes de la Historia Afroamericana	24
Mi colección del centésimo día	17
Mi fiesta de la piñata	126
Mi graduación	75
Mi linterna azul	159
Mi lugar para volar	54
Monedas	56
Neumáticos viejos	148
¡No bromees!	109
No soy un plumcot	62
Nuestra familia	150
Nuestra familia ensamblada	120
Obon	94
Patinetosos Los	128
Pensar en el Día Mundial del Pensamiento	32
perfume de mamá, El	71
¡Perro valiente!	114
¡Piip, piip, piip!	130
poetisa celebra el Mes Nacional de la Sopa, La	10
Preparada para espaguetis	136
Preparamos pan	140
Presentación de la Semana de las Mascotas	66
Primavera	43
primer día de escuela, El	108
primera risa del bebé navajo, La	48
Problema de peso!	52
Puedes llamarme	34

Puedo preguntar y puedo aprender	117
Que comiencen los juegos	92
Querido veterano	146
Quítate el sombrero por el Día del Sombrero	16
Receta para un cumpleaños de mellizos	74
Remedio: tirita adhesiva	123
risa, La	68
Rojo, blanco y azul	81
Rompe un huevo	46
Sandía de Verano	103
señor Cosquillitas, El	113
señor Marmota, El	26
siete velas, Las	163
Solsticio de diciembre	160
Sonidos alegres	129
Sonidos de Deepavali	137
Soy más grande	53
sueño hecho realidad, Un	121
sueño sin hambre, Un	73
Sueños de bicicleta	64
Tan alto como la Montaña Everest	125
Tanka de cumpleaños	22
Tarjeta de Bolsillo	58
Ten cuidado``	106
Tierra, eres	57
tigre, El	156
Tres Reyes Magos	14
Una bicicleta para diez personas	147
Vamos	65
Ven a jugar	143
Verano en Alaska	85
Viva el Día de Acción de Gracias	151
Viva el Día de Año Nuevo	23
Votación	142
¡Wafles, wafles, wafles!	112
¡Yo puedo ayudar!	13
Yoyó	80

Activities, 65, 90
  Baking/Cooking, 87, 100, 132, 140, 141, 151
  Camping, 76
  Crafts, 93, 120
  Dancing, 27, 53, 59, 94, 124, 164
  Drawing, 33, 53, 154
  Jokes, 109
  Photos, 61, 63, 75, 100, 115, 144
  Puzzles/Games, 21, 61, 74, 80, 92, 116, 143, 145, 153, 164
  Shopping, 102, 110
Animals, 14, 26, 41, 44, 52, 67, 76, 78, 106, 107, 127, 131, 156
  Bears, 34, 110, 122, 128
  Birds, 13, 28, 43, 49, 54, 76, 78, 119, 131, 151, 152
  Dinosaurs, 127
  Pets, 28, 66, 113, 114
Behavior, 72, 133, 136, 148
  Kindness, 20, 28, 37, 69, 110, 116
  Love, 22, 28, 29, 61, 71, 81-82, 101, 113, 115, 120, 123, 158-159
  Patriotism, 30, 81, 91, 121, 142, 146
  Thanks, 37, 38, 43, 45, 82, 105, 138, 140, 151
Books and Words, 38, 41, 51, 55, 60, 70, 79, 135, 141
  Bilingual, 27, 29, 31, 48, 60, 81, 115, 122, 134, 137, 140, 144
  Braille, 11
  Letter-writing, 37
  Library, 54, 70, 79, 117, 143, 157
  Multi-lingual, 82, 99
  Poetry, 10, 49, 58
Clothing, 23, 49, 69, 94, 100, 108, 138, 139, 148-149
  Hat, 16, 42, 93, 164
Colors, 25, 42, 77-78, 81, 91, 103, 120, 131, 150, 156, 159, 163
Diversity, 32, 86-87, 120, 150
  African American, 18, 24, 84, 163
  Arab American, 50, 88
  Asian American, 23, 61-62, 87, 94, 118, 137
  Disabilities, 11, 114, 154
  Hispanic American, 31, 59-60, 81, 101, 115, 117, 126, 134, 144
  Native American, 34, 48, 140
Dreams, 12, 18, 36, 59, 64, 73, 121

Family, 32, 35, 45, 46, 48, 61-62, 87, 91, 100-101, 120-121, 140, 141, 144, 150
  Adoption, 35, 150
  Babies/Siblings, 48, 53, 61, 74
  Fathers, 62, 82, 119, 141, 150
  Grandparents, 23, 31, 34, 48, 61-62, 68, 81, 83, 87, 101, 115, 134, 140-141, 144
  Mothers, 13, 31, 48, 62, 71, 86, 123, 137, 141, 150
Food, 32, 39, 45, 49, 58, 73, 88- 91, 116, 127, 136-137, 144-145, 151, 153, 162
  Bread, 119, 134, 140, 144-145
  Breakfast, 73, 88, 112, 131-132
  Desserts/Sweets, 48, 74-75, 87, 98, 100, 103, 105, 126, 132, 138, 155, 158, 162
  Eggs, 46, 131
  Fruits/Vegetables, 62, 77, 102-103
  Pizza, 15, 25
  Popcorn, 19
  Soup, 10
History, 18, 24, 56, 81, 84, 91, 96, 104, 111, 127, 135, 145
  President(s), 30, 56
  Women, 36
Holidays, 42, 138, 151, 162
  Birthdays, 18, 22, 30, 38, 61, 74, 87, 100, 104-105, 113, 126, 139, 152, 165
  Parades, 27, 77, 86, 91
  Religious Holidays, 14, 45-46, 88, 119, 137, 144, 153, 161
Mathematics, 21, 33, 34, 50, 52, 74, 90, 97, 147, 157
  Counting, 17, 76, 152, 164
  Money, 17, 23, 56, 61, 105, 153
  Shapes, 32, 39, 80, 94, 137, 143, 149
Music, 27, 47, 59, 77, 86, 94, 129
Nature, 76
  Earth, 43, 57, 59
  Ecology, 13, 28, 44, 50, 64, 83, 110, 148, 156
  Fire, 130, 140, 156
  Moon, 23, 49, 50, 61, 76, 78, 88, 96, 118
  Mountain, 125

Tree(s), 28, 50, 97, 124, 161
Water, 11, 14, 44, 95, 103, 106, 119, 133, 137
Weather, 26, 43, 85, 152, 159
  People
  Engineers, 33
  Friends, 20, 28, 37, 78, 94, 99, 114, 116, 143, 154
  Helpers, 13, 28, 31, 69, 111, 114
  Scouts, 32
  Veterans, 146
School, 17, 31, 66, 75, 94, 99, 108
  Teachers, 31, 61, 67, 75
Sounds, 19, 27, 46, 59, 66, 68, 76, 86, 92, 98, 104, 129, 130, 137
Sports, 65
  Baseball, 16, 47, 85
  Basketball, 104
  Bicycling, 64, 147
  Football, 25
  Roller-skating, 128
  Swimming, 36, 90
Time/Seasons, 40, 128
  Fall, 40, 118, 124, 128
  New Year, 12, 23, 100, 119, 164
  Spring, 26, 40, 43, 47, 57, 128, 152
  Summer, 79, 85, 90, 103, 128, 160
  Winter, 26, 85, 128, 152, 158, 160-161
Transportation, 33, 35, 49, 64, 83, 111, 114, 147, 154

Acey, Joy, 76

Ada, Alma Flor, 31

Alarcón, Francisco X., 27, 101

Argueta, Jorge, 59

Asher, Sandy, 70

Atkins, Jeannine, 36

Bagert, Brod, 151

Balan, Bruce, 156

Barakat, Ibtisam, 50, 88

Barnes, Michelle Heidenrich, 32, 69

Bennett, Doraine, 120

Bernier-Grand, Carmen T., 14

Black, Robyn Hood, 37

Blackaby, Susan, 96, 131

Bradshaw, Merry, 65

Bruchac, Joseph, 152, 161

Calmenson, Stephanie, 114

Campbell, Robyn, 122

Campoy, F. Isabel, 29

Carlstrom, Nancy White, 51, 85

Cheng, Andrea, 87

Coombs, Kate, 106, 150

Cotten, Cynthia, 155

Dempsey, Kristy, 21, 53, 55

Dotlich, Rebecca Kai, 92

Dryfhout, Linda, 91

Duke, Shirley, 40, 47

Engle, Margarita, 13, 125-126

Esenwine, Matt Forrest, 39

Fineman, Kelly Ramsdell, 56

Finison, Carrie, 136

Flood, Nancy Bo, 48

Florian, Douglas, 97

Franco, Betsy , 17

Gerber, Carole, 38, 82

Ghigna, Charles, 132

Grady, Cynthia, 68

Graham, Joan Bransfield, 16, 139

Grimes, Nikki, 18

Grover, Lorie Ann, 63

Gunning, Monica, 162

Hahn, Mary Lee, 20, 57

Harley, Avis, 127

Harrison, David L., 124

Havill, Juanita, 83

Healy, Jane Heitman, 99

Heard, Georgia, 121

Hemphill, Stephanie, 46

Hershenhorn, Esther, 42

Holbrook, Sara, 95

Hoyte, Carol-Ann, 163

Jules, Jacqueline, 133

Katz, Bobbi, 30

Klostermann, Penny Parker, 149

Krishnaswami, Uma, 137

Krueger, Michele, 77

Larios, Julie, 115

Latham, Irene, 107

LaTulippe, Renée M., 74, 154

Lee, B.J., 129

Levin, Neal, 148

Levinson, Suzy, 33, 130

Lewis, J. Patrick, 34, 113, 147

Lin, Grace, 118

Lyon, George Ella, 44, 80

MacCulloch, Jone Rush, 25

Macken, JoAnn Early, 75

Magee, Bridget, 123

Martinez, Libby, 78, 81

Mayr, Diane, 142

Mora, Pat, 60

Murray, Diana, 79

Nesbitt, Kenn, 12

Newman, Lesléa, 86, 153

Ode, Eric, 66-67

Park, Linda Sue, 23, 61

Patton, Jane Lichtenberger, 43

Paul, Ann Whitford, 105

Prelutsky, Jack, 128

Quattlebaum, Mary, 19

Raczka, Bob, 49

Reese, Debbie, 140

Roemer, Heidi Bee, 52

Rose, Caroline Starr, 160

Rosen, Michael J., 73

Ruddell, Deborah, 108

Salas, Laura Purdie, 89, 93

Saldaña, René Jr., 134, 144

Salinger, Michael, 64

Schaub, Michelle, 15, 109

Schechter, Robert, 41

Scheu, Ted, 54

Sidman, Joyce, 22

Silverman, Buffy, 45, 102

Singer, Marilyn, 165

Slesarik, Ken, 158

Spinelli, Eileen, 10, 28, 72, 159

Steinglass, Elizabeth, 157

Stohr-Hunt, Tricia, 103

Suen, Anastasia, 143, 164

Swanson, Susan Marie, 135

Tahe, Rose Ann, 48

Thompson, Holly, 94

Toht, Patricia, 145

Trout, Linda Kulp, 116, 146

VanDerwater, Amy Ludwig, 138

Wardlaw, Lee , 98, 100

Waters, Charles, 24, 84, 104

Wayland, April Halprin, 110, 119

Wissinger, Tamera Will, 111

Withrow, Steven, 11

Wolf, Allan, 112

Wolff, Virginia Euwer, 141

Wong, Janet, 58, 62, 71, 90, 117

Yolen, Jane, 26, 35

Joy Acey: "Camping"; copyright © 2015 by Joy Acey. Used with permission of the author.

Alma Flor Ada: Bilingual / Bilingüe; copyright © 2015 by Alma Flor Ada. Used with permission of the author.

Francisco X. Alarcón: Carnival Tuesday/Martes de Carnaval, Family Day / Día familiar; copyright © 2015 by Francisco X. Alarcón. Used with permission of the author.

Jorge Argueta: El bailarín/The Dancer; copyright © 2015 by Jorge Argueta. Used with permission of the author.

Sandy Asher: Treasure Hunt; copyright © 2015 by Sandy Asher. Used with permission of the author.

Jeannine Atkins: A Long Time Ago; copyright © 2015 by Jeannine Atkins. Used with permission of the author.

Brod Bagert: A Thanksgiving Cheer; copyright © 2015 by Brod Bagert. Used with permission of the author.

Bruce Balan: Tiger; copyright © 2015 by Bruce Balan. Used with permission of the author.

Ibtisam Barakat: Tree Day Celebration, "Break-Fast" at Night; copyright © 2015 by Ibtisam Barakat. Used with permission of the author.

Michelle Heidenrich Barnes: Thinking about World Thinking Day, Look for the Helpers; copyright © 2015 by Michelle Heidenrich Barnes. Used with permission of the author.

Doraine Bennett: Our Blended Family; copyright © 2015 by Doraine Bennett. Used with permission of the author.

Carmen T. Bernier-Grand: Three Kings Day/Tres Reyes Magos; copyright © 2015 by Carmen T. Bernier-Grand. Used with permission of the author.

Robyn Hood Black: Sincerely; copyright © 2015 by Robyn Hood Black. Used with permission of the author.

Susan Blackaby: Moon Walk—July 21, 1969, World Egg Day; copyright © 2015 by Susan Blackaby. Used with permission of the author.

Merry Bradshaw: Let's Go; copyright © 2015 by Merry Bradshaw. Used with permission of the author.

Joseph Bruchac: Winter Counting, Christmas Tree; copyright © 2015 by Joseph Bruchac. Used with permission of the author.

Stephanie Calmenson: Brave Dog!; copyright © 2015 by Stephanie Calmenson. Used with permission of the author.

Robyn Campbell: Pirate Talk; copyright © 2015 by Robyn Campbell. Used with permission of the author.

F. Isabel Campoy: Bilingual Daisy/Margarita bilingüe; copyright © 2015 by F. Isabel Campoy. Used with permission of the author.

Nancy White Carlstrom: Books, Summer in Alaska; copyright © 2015 by Nancy White Carlstrom. Used with permission of the author.

Andrea Cheng: Wishes Around the World; copyright © 2015 by Andrea Cheng. Used with permission of Curtis Brown, Ltd.

Kate Coombs: Beware, Our Family by Kate Coombs; copyright © 2015 by Kate Coombs. Used with permission of the author.

Cynthia Cotten: Cookies!; copyright © 2015 by Cynthia Cotten. Used with permission of the author.

Kristy Dempsey: 100 Pieces, I'm Bigger, STOP! Let's Read!; copyright © 2015 by Kristy Dempsey. Used with permission of the author.

Rebecca Kai Dotlich: Let the Games Begin; copyright © 2015 by Rebecca Kai Dotlich. Used with permission of Curtis Brown, Ltd.

Linda Dryfhout: Independence Day; copyright © 2015 by Linda Dryfhout. Used with permission of the author.

Shirley Duke: Daylight Saving Time, Baseball's Opening Day; copyright © 2015 by Shirley Duke. Used with permission of the author.

Margarita Engle: I Can Help! /¡Yo puedo ayudar!, As High as Mount Everest/Tan Alto Como la Montaña Everest, My Piñata Party/Mi Fiesta de la Piñata; copyright © 2015 by Margarita Engle. Used with permission of the author.

Matt Forrest Esenwine: Picky Eater; copyright © 2015 by Matt Forrest Esenwine. Used with permission of the author.

Kelly Ramsdell Fineman: Pocket Change; copyright © 2015 by Kelly Ramsdell Fineman. Used with permission of the author.

Carrie Finison: Ready for Spaghetti; copyright © 2015 by Carrie Finison. Used with permission of the author.

Nancy Bo Flood: First Laugh, Navajo Baby; copyright © 2015 by Nancy Bo Flood. Used with permission of the author.

Douglas Florian: National Hammock Day; copyright © 2015 by Douglas Florian. Used with permission of the author.

Betsy Franco: My 100th Day Collection; copyright © 2015 by Betsy Franco. Used with permission of the author.

Carole Gerber: Happy Birthday, Dr. Seuss, A Day to Honor Fathers; copyright © 2015 by Carole Gerber. Used with permission of the author.

Charles Ghigna: The Day After National Dessert Day; copyright © 2015 by Charles Ghigna. Used with permission of the author.

Cynthia Grady: Laughing; copyright © 2015 by Cynthia Grady. Used with permission of the author.

Joan Bransfield Graham: Hats Off to Hat Day, Birthday; copyright © 2015 by Joan Bransfield Graham. Used with permission of the author.

COPYRIGHT & PERMISSIONS

For permission to reprint any of the poems in this book, please contact the individual poets listed here either directly or through their agents. Most of these poets can be reached through their individual websites, which are listed at our Pomelo Books website, PomeloBooks.com. If you need help getting in touch with a poet, just let us know and we'll be happy to connect you. A note on copyright:

If it doesn't feel right to copy it . . . please don't!

Poets (like plumbers and lawyers and teachers and acrobats) need to earn a living from their work; permissions fees and royalties help pay the rent!

Biographical information, photos, and lists of some of the published titles of each of our contributing poets can be found at PomeloBooks.com. Younger children might like to know, for instance, that Jack Prelutsky collects frog miniatures and April Halprin Wayland was once an aqua farmer! On the Web you'll find contact info for the poets as well as news about their books and links to their blogs. If you identified "favorite poets" when reading the poems in this anthology, you might want to contact them about speaking at your school or library—either in person or via video chat—or participating in a conference or workshop. Some poets enjoy large assemblies, some prefer small sessions, and some do both. Contact them and start a conversation!

ACKNOWLEDGMENTS

It was very important—and not a simple task—to "get the Spanish right." We were fortunate to have the guidance and counsel of Alma Flor Ada and F. Isabel Campoy from the very start of our project. Their glowing recommendation of our lead translator Liliana Cosentino gave us the confidence we needed at the beginning of this project, and we so appreciate the many hours they spent working together to refine translations. We also are extremely grateful for the close reading and editorial support provided by Jennifer and Jenny Barillas, David Bowles, and Julie Larios; Cynthia Alaniz, Consuelo Avila, Silvia Zulema Bewley, Xelena Gonzalez, Brenda Linares, Juanita Vega, and Karim Zomar; and other readers who shared their time and expertise. Thank you, too, to Renée M. LaTulippe and Emily Vardell for editorial assistance and research.

A final note: our thanks to our readers and book buyers and book sharers for their support. Please visit our blogs and website and continue to spread the word about our books!

ABOUT THE AUTHORS

Sylvia M. Vardell is Professor in the School of Library and Information Studies at Texas Woman's University and has taught graduate courses in children's and young adult literature at various universities since 1981. Vardell has published extensively, including five books on literature for children, as well as over 25 book chapters and 100 journal articles. Her current work focuses on poetry for children, including a regular blog, PoetryforChildren, since 2006.

Janet S. Wong is a graduate of Yale Law School and a former lawyer who switched careers and became a children's poet. Her dramatic career change has been featured on *The Oprah Winfrey Show* and other shows. She is the author of 30 books for children and teens on a wide variety of subjects.

Praise for *The Poetry Friday Anthology* Series

K-5 Poetry

"Find a place for this book on your desk since you'll be turning to it time and time again."

— Barbara Ward, *IRA's Reading Today*

"This is a lot of resource and professional development for $29.99!"

— Jeanette Larson, from *The ALSC Blog*

"It's a *vade mecum* for the elementary teacher and a word magnet for the K-5 child. Brava to the anthologists and the poets!"

— J. Patrick Lewis
Poetry Foundation Children's Poet Laureate

Middle School Poetry

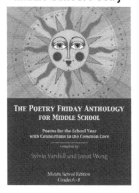

"The Common Core standards provided throughout the book **give teachers confidence that they are integrating key skills** as they share the poems. The book highlights and documents specific skills and techniques, such as rhyme, repetition, rhythm, and alliteration, as they are used one poem at a time."

— *U.S. Kids Magazine (Parents & Teachers)*

K-5 Science Poetry Teacher or Student Editions

"Savvy teachers have learned they can trust Vardell and Wong."

— *IRA's Reading Today*

"The greatest science poetry ever written for children, with a twist—"

— *NSTA Recommends*

For more information about *The Poetry Friday Anthology* series, please visit **PomeloBooks.com**.

Praise for *You Just Wait: A Poetry Friday Power Book*

YOU JUST WAIT: *A Poetry Friday Power Book* for tweens and teens, features 12 PowerPack sets that combine:

12 poems from ***The Poetry Friday Anthology for Middle School***

24 new original Response Poems and Mentor Texts

12 **PowerPlay** prewriting activities

and 12 **Power2You** writing prompts

PowerPacks = a fun and inspiring approach for a wide variety of readers and writers! **Grades 4 and up.**

"Imagine **a completely original way of writing** verse novellas . . . "
—Margarita Engle, Newbery Honor-winning author of *The Surrender Tree*

"*YOU JUST WAIT* is **a must-have resource for middle-school** teachers, the perfect invitation for teens to explore text-to-self connections through poetry."
—David Bowles, Pura Belpré Honor-winning author of *The Smoking Mirror*

"Great spirit! Great fun! Let's write!"
—Pat Mora, Author of *Dizzy in Your Eyes: Poems about Love*; Founder of Día: Children's Day, Book Day / El día de los niños, El día de los libros

"Young readers will find their fingers itching to respond to these verses and to add their own poems and stories."
—Carol Jago, Longtime English teacher & Past President of NCTE (National Council of Teachers of English)

For free downloadable samples of *You Just Wait*, including **PowerPlay** prewriting activities, Response Poems, Mentor Texts, and **Power2You** writing prompts, please visit **PomeloBooks.com**.

Made in the USA
Columbia, SC
11 January 2018